Uncle Phil
and the Atomic Bomb

Uncle Phil
and the Atomic Bomb

John Abelson
Philip H. Abelson

ROBERTS AND COMPANY
GREENWOOD VILLAGE, COLORADO

Roberts and Company Publishers
4950 South Yosemite Street, F2 #197
Greenwood Village, Colorado 80111 USA
Internet: www.roberts-publishers.com
Telephone: (303) 221-3325
Facsimile: (303) 221-3326

ORDER INFORMATION
Telephone: (800) 351-1161 or (516) 422-4050
Facsimile: (516) 422-4097
Internet: www.roberts-publishers.com

Publisher: Ben Roberts
Copyeditors: John Murdzek and Gunder Hefta
Interior and cover design: Mark Ong
Compositor: Side by Side Studios

ISBN: 0-9747077-7-5

Library of Congress Cataloging-in-Publication Data

Abelson, Philip Hauge.
  Uncle Phil and the atomic bomb / by Philip H. Abelson and John Abelson.
    p. cm.
  ISBN 0-9747077-7-5
  1. Abelson, Philip Hauge. 2. Physicists--United States--Biography. 3. Scientists--United States--Biography. I. Abelson, John. II. Title.
  QC16.A255A3 2007
  621.48092--dc22
  [B]
                    2007028443

Contents

Preface

Atomic fission was discovered by the group of Hahn, Meitner and Strassman in Berlin just before World War II. The implications of this discovery were immediately clear to physicists everywhere. The enormous energy of the atomic nucleus could be unleashed (at least in part) in the fission reaction. It seemed feasible, moreover, that fission could become a chain reaction under the right conditions. If an atomic bomb could be constructed, its predicted potency would vastly exceed that of conventional explosives.

Before World War II, Germany was the center of the world in physics. As the likelihood of war became evident in 1939, it was apparent to all physicists that Germany had the intellectual and industrial capability to build an atomic bomb. Physicists in the United States and England, many of them refugees from Germany, convinced the allied leadership of the implied danger—namely, the first nation to build an atomic bomb could dictate terms to the rest of the world. President Roosevelt and Prime Minister Churchill deserve credit for taking this threat seriously. Thus, huge financial and intellectual capacity was dedicated to building an atomic bomb in what became known as the Manhattan Project.

The Manhattan Project was principally carried out in three locations: Los Alamos, New Mexico, where the bomb was designed under the direction of Robert Oppenheimer; Oak Ridge, Tennessee, where the fissionable isotope of uranium, ^{235}U, was separated from the predominate (and non-fissionable) isotope, ^{238}U; and Hanford, Washington, where plutonium (a fissionable element) was purified. The project was organized and controlled by the U.S. Army under the overall direction of General Leslie Groves.

Despite the early allied commitment to the atomic bomb project, it was the middle of 1943 before the Manhattan Project got underway on a large scale. By early 1944, the huge plant in Oak Ridge, constructed to separate ^{235}U, began to function, yet early runs were a disaster. It seemed possible that the project to build a uranium bomb could fail. At this point, Robert Oppenheimer learned of a separate atomic energy project being carried out by the Navy at the Naval Research Laboratory in Washington, DC. A small group there, motivated originally by the possibility that atomic energy could power submarines, had developed an independent and unique method for purifying ^{235}U and they were having some success with their approach. Thus, the decision was made to employ this method at Oak Ridge as well. Ultimately, the atomic bomb dropped on Hiroshima on August 6, 1945 contained uranium purified by a tandem process made possible by the Navy effort.

The principal scientist in the Navy effort was my uncle, Philip Abelson. By himself he had initiated the project to purify ^{235}U prior to his association with the Navy. When Uncle Phil left the Navy in 1947, he was less than 35 years old, and yet what he had done was legendary. How could the son of immigrant Norwegians have accomplished so much? I decided I wanted to find out. I knew generally of his contributions to the atomic bomb project, but not through conversations with him. For many years after the war, the details of what he had done were classified, and even after they were released, Uncle Phil was reluctant to discuss them. Rather, as editor of *Science* magazine for many years, his concern was with current science and with prospects for the future, so that was what we discussed.

Then, in 2001 at the annual garden party of the National Academy of Sciences in Washington, DC, my wife Christine Guthrie and I sat in the library with Uncle Phil. We began to question him about his past and were enthralled by his stories. This inspired us to collect an oral history. We enlisted the help of Chris's uncle, Edward Miller, a distinguished naval historian in Washington. (Unbeknownst to us at the time, Amy Crumpton of the American Association for the Advancement of Science was also taking an oral history.) As I listened to the resulting tapes, however, I began to realize that our effort had not begun early enough. His past-told stories had become myths from which the all-important details had been lost.

Then, in 2003, I attended a celebration of Uncle Phil's 90th birthday held at the Carnegie Institution of Washington. When I visited him in his office at the American Association for the Advancement of Science (AAAS), he rummaged in a file drawer and silently handed me several manuscripts, including an extensive autobiographical sketch. I had not known this remarkable document existed. It had been written at least 20 years earlier and had a degree of detail and originality not found in the oral histories. The autobiography was neatly typed and well edited, a sure sign that Aunt Neva, Phil's wife (who was by then deceased), had helped him with it. Phil did not type and all of the editorials he had written for *Science* were typed and creatively edited by Neva. The autobiography had rich details about the family history and Phil's education through the period in Lawrence's lab in Berkeley, but ended before the beginning of World War II. Only in much later speeches and in the oral histories did he talk about the atomic bomb project.

In this book I have let Phil tell his own story (with only minor editing) via his autobiographical manuscript and through later talks and oral histories. Little interpolation or explanation is necessary in the early chapters, but as he arrives in Lawrence's lab much more corroborative and parallel history is available, so I have attempted to supply that through my voice and via other letters and accounts. This becomes especially true in the war years, where he said little and what he did say was understated. My voice in this book is in a smaller font and separated by a line.

Uncle Phil's one sibling, my father Harold, died in 1955 when I was 16, but Phil lived on for almost 50 more years. For me, then, my father was mostly myth and Uncle Phil more real, yet what I knew about Phil before I undertook this project did not fully explain who he was. I understand him better now. The following letter to his mother on the occasion of his 23rd birthday is revealing. He had great self-confidence and large aspirations. In a short time he accomplished more than he could have predicted and indeed did go on to have "his finger in many a scientific pie."

Dear Ma:

Tomorrow I shall be twenty-three years old. Almost one-third of my life expectancy is in the past. The years are beginning to slip by at an ever accelerating pace. In a few years youth with its so carefree days will be gone to be replaced with increasing responsibilities of manhood. However, I do get more and more wary every day about being in a haste to assume the responsibilities of marriage. Other responsibilities, though, are ever on the increase.

As I look back upon my life as it has been lived, I am not dissatisfied. I have lived a rather exceptional life—very few people have as much of experience and success to show for at twenty-three. A lot has come because of the fine heritage of mind and body that was given to me. The rest has come because I've fought and battled for it.

At the same time I have been free from misfortunes. There are many pitfalls and dangers in wait for youth. Very few come through youth unscathed. Somehow I have managed to come through that dangerous period unharmed. Now I have the background of experience both of myself and of some of my less fortunate acquaintances. I know the dangers, their consequences and how to avoid them.

I think I have come through the most dangerous and troubled period of life. From now on there will be much more tranquility and satisfaction in living.

Life as it enfolds will hold an ever changing array of extremely interesting experiences. I will have my hand in many a scientific pie. By the time life is over I will know about as much on the whole broad field of science as anyone. I will have been connected with Scientific Institutions in all corners of the earth. I won't accumulate money. I'll accumulate knowledge and experience. The adventurous spirits of a thousand years ago might seek to learn what was beyond the horizon. They wanted to be living life under changing circumstances. Today, there are no physical horizons, but there are greater and broader intellectual "new lands." In me there has always been an extreme thirst for change, for the new, for far lands. Certainly if I had lived in the days a thousand years ago I would have been one of Leif Ericson's henchmen. Since I am living now, I find that there are even greater things to see and do. And my restless, driving spirit leads me ever in search of new and greater knowledge.

Always, I feel grateful to my parents for the fine start they have given me in life. Few people are brought up and started in life with such a good beginning. I am grateful too, for their continued aid which has certainly made life very satisfactory. A few dollars can make the difference between being pinched and being comfortable. Hope you are well,

Love,

Your Son Phil

This letter was written at least 40 years before the autobiography and before any of his successes. He met most of the goals he set for himself, but he was insufficiently wary about marriage. Within six months he was married to Neva.

Acknowledgements

This book was made possible by the autobiographical sketch prepared by my Uncle Phil. However, he had not envisioned that this document would be published and I take full responsibility for the contents of the book.

I thank my cousin, Ellen Cherniavsky, Phil's daughter, for her support and help in the preparation of the book and for contributing a number of family photographs and letters.

Thanks to Edward Miller and Amy Crumpton for their valuable oral histories.

I very much enjoyed my conversations with Harry and Ellen Weaver, Phil's Oak Ridge friends and for their written recollection of that period. I received helpful comments from Joseph-James Ahern, David Goodstein, Tom Tombrello and Peter Vogel.

I am very grateful to Ben Roberts, the publisher, for his interest and support of this project and to John Murdzek for his careful editing of the manuscript. The book was designed by Mark Ong and Susan Riley of Side by Side Studios in San Francisco.

Finally I thank my wife, Christine Guthrie for her patient support during this long project.

John Abelson

1

An Immigrant Family Succeeds in the New World

My father was born on January 7, 1878, in the ancestral home close by the end of Holandsfjord in Nordland, Norway. The fjord is located north of the Arctic Circle. The soil is rocky on the hillside on which the house and barn are perched. During the short growing season, barley and other cereal grasses could be raised, and a few cows could find forage. A major summer occupation was to cut grass and to make hay for the cows. The principal source of food was codfish, which were abundant near the Lofoten Islands. The fishermen reached the islands in small sailing boats. The sea was often stormy, and many men lost their lives at sea. My father said that his father told him that he had decided to bring the family to America because he wanted a dry grave.

I know little about the racial mix of my father's people. He certainly was no blond Nordic type. In fact, he had black hair, brown eyes, and a stocky build. In 1960, I visited the ancestral farm. On returning on a plane from Bodo, I sat beside a woman anthropologist who had spent many summers in Lapland living with the Lapps (or the Samit, as they prefer to be called). She stared at me searchingly and then told me that my facial features were like those she had noted among the people of Lapland, which is near Holandsfjord.

My father had another story about ancestors. He said that, in times far past, members of the Hanseatic League had used northern Norway as a place to dispose of people who had offended them. They would sail fairly close to shore and fling the unlucky offenders into the icy waters. Some would manage to swim to shore.

While I was at Holandsfjord, one of the residents pointed out important features of the ancestral home and barn. Much of the barn was made of large rocks that only a very strong man could have moved. The barn, which had been built on three levels, nestled against the hillside. On the top level, the hay was brought in. On the middle level dwelt the cows; the hay could be dropped down to them. On the lower level, the manure accumulated. Bacteriological action in the manure produced some heat, which helped to keep the cows from freezing in cold weather. My informant pointed to the logs in the barn. They were relics from a distant past. The trees from which they came no longer grew in northern Norway and had not done so for a long time. In 1960, life had become easier in Holandsfjord. Potatoes and currants were being grown there, and the government had provided electricity to the people of the area.

In 1889, my family immigrated to America, arriving in Baltimore. The group included Grandfather Lars, Grandmother Anna, Uncle Alfred (about two years older than my father Olaf Andreas), Aunt Marie, Aunt Ethel, and Aunt Anna. Uncle Emil, who was the oldest son, stayed for a time in Norway. My Uncle Edwin was born after the family had settled in Minnesota.

The first days in the United States were unhappy ones. In the great land of opportunity, there were robbers who preyed on non-English-speaking immigrants. On the train west from Baltimore, Grandfather was chloroformed and robbed of all the family's money. Thus, they arrived penniless in northern Minnesota with winter fast approaching. That winter, they lived in a sod hut.

In due course, Grandfather obtained a homestead of 160 acres in the Red River Valley near Crookston and Warren, Minnesota. Life was hard there, but the family managed. In about 1895, though, when my father was 17, Grandfather died. Responsibility for running the farm and supporting the family fell to my father. He plowed the land using a team of oxen. There were cows to milk and chickens and turkeys to attend to. In the winter, he went to school, and he completed the eighth grade. At that time and place, an eighth-grade education was sufficient to enable a man to teach school, so he became a schoolteacher.

Most of his efforts in his late teens and early twenties, however, were devoted to the farm. There he encountered frequent
bitter disappointments. In addition to various forms of crop failure, there were prairie fires. Once, a violent summer storm
drenched the turkeys, and they all got sick and died. The continu-
ing travail made a deep impression on him. Forty years later he
would report at breakfast about every two weeks that he had had
"that dream" of the turkey catastrophe on the farm.

Much of my father's account of his early life was told to me
on a single occasion when I was about 10 years old. Naturally,
there were gaps in the story. One was of events in the years
roughly between 1900 and 1905. In that period, his sisters reached
maturity, and there was no longer so heavy a burden of family
support. He never went to high school, but he managed to learn
most or all of the material necessary to be admitted to college. In
those days, formal requirements were not rigid, but he must have
mastered algebra and geometry by studying at home.

Sometime during that 1900–1905 interval, he attended the
University of North Dakota at Grand Forks. It was the custom in
those days for sophomores to haze the freshmen. Father and a
fellow student from Iceland were particular objects of attention.
They were "hayseeds" without evident culture. The two were
drawn together by the hazing and by language; the Norwegian
spoken in Nordland is very close to Icelandic, so the two teamed
together. When a group of sophomores bent on hazing next

approached them, Father held off most of them while the Icelander lifted one high above his head and flung him to the ground. That was the end of the hazing. My impression is that Father's attendance at the University of North Dakota was limited to one year.

Also during that period, probably in 1903 or 1904, my father met my mother, Ellen Hauge. I was never told much about the courtship. My mother said, on several occasions, that she had received many letters from my father that included much romantic poetry that he had written.

My knowledge of my mother's early years is limited. She was born in Skjolden, Norway, on October 20, 1882. Skjolden is at the easternmost end of Sogne Fjord, which is an important and scenic area of Norway, located at about latitude 61° in the southern third of the country. The climate is sufficiently mild that fruit trees, such as apples, can be grown there.

The Hauges were fairly prosperous people. (My former associate Merle Tuve once told me that the Hauges ruled Norway for five hundred years. That may or may not be true. In any event, the ancestry can be traced.)[1] Distinguished people have had their roots in the area of Sogne Fjord. Former Vice-President Walter Mondale's people came from a branch of the fjord known as

---

[1] "Luster", Jon Laerberg, A.S John Griegs Boktrykkeri, Bergen, 1926.

Mon Dahl. The family of Norman Borlaug (the recipient of the 1970 Nobel Peace Prize and so-called father of the Green Revolution) also came from the fjord, not very far from Skjolden. Merle told me that, because of the geometry and isolation of the area, everyone in Sogne Fjord was related. He estimated that we were probably at least fourth cousins.

My mother had many brothers and sisters. She never told me much about her childhood or adolescence. One set of experiences she did mention on a number of occasions was that of tending cows during the summertime. High above the fjord in the mountains, the grass was luxuriant during the summer. The family had living quarters there. She called the place the Saeter. The cows gave a peak output of milk that was converted to butter and cheese. Ma had fond memories of the Saeter, particularly the beauty of the surroundings. When I visited her birthplace in 1960, I went for a climb in the mountains above the fjord. The scenery was magnificent and ever-changing as small clouds moved across the scene.

At age 18, my mother decided to emigrate to America. Sogne Fjord was close to being overpopulated. She wanted her children to have better opportunities than they could have near her birthplace. It was a courageous decision for a girl so young to leave home, relatives, and friends to go alone to a strange land. She did have the advantage of knowing some people who had earlier emigrated to North Dakota, and she could stay with them as a first stop. It is unclear where she obtained the money to make the journey. Her family lived comfortably, but they were not rich. After she arrived in North Dakota, she worked. What she did was probably housework, but what really matters was that she was able to save some of the money she earned.

My parents were married in 1905, and they proceeded to Pullman, Washington, with the plan of attending the State College of Washington (now Washington State University). They arrived well ahead of the beginning of the school year. They bought land on what is now part of the campus and they built a house. The grantee deed to the property, which cost $100, was in my mother's name; when the property was sold to Washington State College both parents' names appeared as grantors.[2]

They had enough money to pay for land and building materials, but there was not much more. Both of them registered as students. When they had paid for registration and for the necessary books, the family treasury held only six dollars. They took in a boarder, and Mother served as a waitress in the college commons. They worked and they studied. Both had very good grades. Mother took a general course, and Father studied civil engineering.

---

[2] The house no longer exists, but it was very near the Biology Building, which has since been named Abelson Hall in honor of Phil and Neva.

During weekends and in the summers, Father worked part of the time as a harvest hand in the wheat fields nearby. He told one story about working for the college. At that time, the school was growing, and new buildings were being constructed. This meant that ditches needed to be dug for water pipes and sewer lines. The college had found that the usual student help did more leaning on their shovels and talking than digging, so they established a wage scale based on how many feet of ditch were dug. When the authorities discovered how much ditch Father had dug in his first two weeks on the job, they were horrified. He had earned an amount that was on the level of their most highly paid professors. The so-and-sos immediately renegotiated the pay scale.

My brother, Harold, was born January 1, 1908. That necessarily ended my mother's attendance at college. But both of my parents had fond memories of Washington State. They had respect especially for Enoch Bryan, who had been an eloquent and successful college president during their time as students there.

After graduation in June, 1909, the family moved to Tacoma. My father's brothers and sisters had gone there along with their mother. Father sought work as a civil engineer, but none was immediately available. He worked as a carpenter, and he bought lots and erected a home at 2204 East 35th Street. He told me that, as time went on and he could not find employment as a civil engineer, he thought sadly of the struggle to earn his bachelor's degree. Finally, though, he obtained a position in 1912, and throughout the rest of his life was employed as a civil engineer.

His first job as an engineer was for the American Smelting and Refining Company, which had a big smelter and refinery on the north side of Tacoma. When he was hired, it was to help in the design of a 576-foot-high smokestack. He had taken courses in the design of reinforced concrete structures in college. This was a relatively new engineering development, and he made himself particularly useful.[3]

Thus, the family was at last in good financial and professional circumstances by April 27, 1913, when I was born. My birth was regarded as a particularly happy event. I have often meditated about the contrast of the circumstances at the time of my brother's birth and at the time of my own. To some extent, his arrival at an awkward time must have influenced parental attitudes, particularly those of my mother. She never made any remark about it, but it seemed that I was the fair-haired boy, and Harold was often in bad odor. Much later, the relationship between my mother and Harold improved.

(In this book I will occasionally make interpolations or additions. My voice will appear in a smaller font as seen below. —JA)

By the time this was written, the competition between Phil and my father Harold for their mother's love was long over. I am

---

[3] The smokestack survived for many years and was the most notable feature of the Tacoma skyline but, some 20 years ago, with the smelter no longer in use, the smokestack was destroyed.

not sure when the relationship between my father and his mother improved, but presumably it had by the end of their lives. In 1953 my father, a civil engineer like his father, was appointed resident engineer by the City of Tacoma. He was hired to build two dams on the Cowlitz River, so our family moved from Priest River, Idaho to Tacoma in early 1955. This was the most important job my father held and would have been the pinnacle of his career. He was not in good health, though. He had been a heavy smoker and had pleurisy. In addition, Grandmother Ellen was dying of cancer. That winter my father often spent evenings at her house. The strain of the move, the new job, and the burden of caring for his mother proved to be too much for him. He died in February 1955 two days before she did. He was 47 years old; she was 73.

Whatever disagreements my parents may have had were settled privately. Never in all the years that I was with them did they argue or even disagree in my presence. My mother had reservations about her in-laws and about some of what she considered the sometimes over-exuberant behavior of my father.[4] But, insofar as she acted to restrain him, it was done quietly, behind the scenes. After my father's death in 1939, I learned of some events in which she had disapproved of his actions. These came at the time when I was born. My father was very happy when I arrived—so much so that he wanted to name me Felix (Latin for "happy"). I suspect that, in part, he wanted to remind

---

[4] My wife has the same concerns about me, so over-exuberance may be an inherited trait.

The Abelson Family in about 1916:
Harold (left), Ellen, Olaf (in back), and Philip (right).

the neighbors that he had a college education. He was also sufficiently pleased with his new son that he invited all and sundry to
come see the baby. The net result was that, in my first month of
life, I contracted pneumonia, measles, and chickenpox. In due
course, those problems were overcome, but the disagreement
about the name endured longer. By the time I entered grade
school, my mother had succeeded in devising a compromise:
Philip, which is an unlikely name for a person of Norwegian
descent. However, it had some flavor of scholarship, reminding
one of Philip of Macedonia, father of Alexander the Great.

The final episode in the contest of the name came in 1941. I
had become an employee of the Naval Research Laboratory in
Washington, DC, and security-clearance procedures required a
copy of my birth certificate. I asked my mother to go to the courthouse and get one for me. When she did, she discovered that my
official name was still Felix. She later let me know, very quietly,
that seeing that name on the certificate had made her angry all
over again.[5]

In 1917, as war approached, the smelting company needed
an engineer at its big smelter in Garfield, Utah. The smelter was
about 40 miles from Salt Lake City, and it was not far from the

---

[5] By this time, my grandfather was dead (he had passed away in 1939), and Grandmother
Ellen apparently got in the last word by going to the courthouse and officially changing
Felix to Philip.

lake itself. About five miles from Garfield was the Bingham Canyon copper deposit, one of the greatest in the world.

Circumstances in Garfield in 1917 were not salubrious. In those days, smoke coming out of stacks was looked upon with favor. It was a symbol of prosperity and well-paying jobs. But the sulfur dioxide spewing from the stacks at Garfield meant more than prosperity. It was an air pollutant that destroyed the vegetation of the surrounding area. Neither grass nor trees grew in Garfield. This was particularly saddening to my mother, who loved flowers and scenes of natural beauty. The other drawback of Utah at that time was the attitude of the Mormons to people of other religious faiths. We were Methodists, and among the Mormons were known as "Gentiles." The Mormons, who were in the overwhelming majority, were particularly hostile to Gentiles.

About 20 years previously, the federal government had abolished polygamy in Utah, and bitterness about this action prevailed. Consequently, our family, and particularly the boys, lived in a hostile environment.

In this situation, my father found it advisable to be courteous to the pairs of Mormon missionaries who often came calling, seeking to make converts. My mother would have nothing to do with them. He gave them sufficient encouragement that he and I (no more than five years old) were invited to visit the Mormon Tabernacle in Salt Lake City. We were ushered into the place, and as we approached the Holy of Holies, guards at the entrance asked, "Are they Saints?" Our hosts responded, "No, but they are going to be." And so we went into the Holy of Holies.

I established a relationship with the young Mormons in another way. One day I wandered some distance from home and was suddenly surrounded by a gang. They selected one of their number to beat up on me. I responded with such vigor and ferocity that my assailant went home crying. Thereafter, I was accepted as an honorary Mormon, and I was welcomed by boys several years older than I to participate in their activities. Because I was five years younger than my brother, I did not move in his circles. However, he also apparently found his own mode of living comfortably among the Mormons.

Once the war was over, on November 11, 1918, my mother campaigned for us to return to Tacoma. She longed for the beauty of Puget Sound and the mountains and for a place where she could have flowers. In fact, she had argued against going to Utah in the first place. She had said, "If we move to this new place, we will set a pattern for our sons. They will get itchy feet. They will later move from place to place and spend their lives traveling." My mother's wishes were fulfilled. By April, 1919, we were back in our home in Tacoma.[6]

From 1919 through 1929, I lived exclusively at 2204 East Thirty-fifth Street, and during that interval assembled a rich store

---

[6] Grandmother Ellen's prediction about traveling was true for my father Harold. He built hydroelectric dams in the West, and we moved every three years from 1941 to 1955.

of pleasant memories. Every prospect was pleasing. There was a happy family life. The national mood was one of great progress and prosperity. Our home was situated at the edge of the city. We were only about three miles from the center of the city, but, within a mile, there was second-growth timber, open prairie, scores of different kinds of birds, many wild animals, and a swimming hole. The weather was mild. There were rain and fog in the winter, but the temperature was rarely below freezing. We had a cow, chickens, and a garden.

There were enough chores for a boy to feel that he was a useful member of the family, but there were not so many as to interfere unduly with all kinds of wide-ranging activities. One of my

The house at 2204 East Thirty-fifth Street, Tacoma, as it appears today.

main chores was taking care of the wood supply. In summer, we had delivered four or five big truckloads of wood slabs that were by-products of local sawmills. The wood was wet, and it had to be piled for drying. Later, it was thrown through windows into the basement, where it was again piled. The dry wood was split as necessary, and it supplied fuel for cooking and home heating. Whatever the chores I was assigned, I completed them with dispatch and without grumbling. Then I usually proceeded to go alone on some exploration of the woods or to play with one or more of the neighbor boys.

School was easy for me. Before I entered the first grade, I could read and also do some adding and multiplying. Our eight-year grade school (Roosevelt) had only six classrooms, so that as many as three different grades—for example, 1B, 1A, and 2B—were present in one room. My practice was to complete my assignments quickly and then to listen to the teacher as she taught the others. I enjoyed learning, a pleasure that was reinforced by knowing that I was the best student in the class. The teachers saw fit to give me double promotions, so I completed the eight grades in six and a half years. After that, I attended the newly built Franklin B. Gault Intermediate School for ninth grade and Lincoln High School for the remainder of my secondary education. My performance in grades 9 through 12 was not particularly sparkling. I did finish high school third among the boys in a class of 400, though. I had difficulty with the first semester of geometry, in part because I did not like the teacher. I did well the second semester with a different teacher. A year of high-school physics lit no fires. However, a half-year of chemistry during my final semester of high school rang bells with me. The teacher, Miss Florence Kelly, was a warm woman who knew how to teach.

My physical growth pattern affected my relationship with school and classmates. I was slow to have my adolescent growth spurt. This, combined with being in classes with older students, made me a peewee among those who had attained the major part of their adult stature. Another factor was my reticence—perhaps even bashfulness. In addition, while I was physically active, I was not gifted as an athlete—just average. Thus, during the first two years in high school, I did not participate in social or school activities. During my senior year, however, I became more active. I had been a patriotic attendee of high-school games. Our principal rival at that time was Stadium High School. It was the school attended by the children of the well-to-do. Ours was the school of those less well-off.

I decided that I could not contribute athletically, but that I could at least be on the staff of the high-school weekly paper. During the first semester of my senior year, I took a course in journalism; in the second semester, I served on the paper. I read copy, wrote headlines, and contributed a few pieces, including an editorial. I attended sessions at the printer's in the evening while last-minute adjustments were made prior to the press run. The experience was a very useful introduction to techniques of communication.

An important part of my education took place at home. My mother was thoughtful and unusually self-disciplined. She preached "moderation in all things." Neighbors came to consult her when they had problems. They could reveal their secrets to her knowing that they would get good advice and that she would not gossip about them. My father consulted her about business matters. A family saying was, "Pa proposes; Ma disposes." She spoke often about college and about her admiration for Enoch Bryan, who was the president of Washington State College while the family was in Pullman. My mother and I were especially close. She took a switch to me only once. That was after she spotted me atop a pole carrying electrical wires. The rest of the time, I was her fair-haired boy. When the wild flowers were blooming in the spring, I would bring her bouquets. When the wild berries were ripe, I would gather them for her. My mother was deeply religious, and she asked me to accompany her to missions and to annual camp meetings. I was not persuaded by the evangelists, but went with her without complaint.

It is curious that Grandmother Ellen rejected the Lutheran Church of her childhood and embraced an evangelical branch of the Methodist church. It fits, however, with the fact that Norwegian was never spoken in her house. She apparently wanted to put Norway behind her and to become an American. In visits to Tacoma as a child, I often accompanied her to church and also to prayer meetings during the week. With the exception of Grandmother Ellen, who was reserved and circumspect, the participants in these meetings were highly emotional, sometimes talking in tongues. I squirmed in my seat and read the hymnal. The endless prayer meetings were particularly tedious.

I spent less time with my father than with my mother, but the relationship was a good one. On Saturdays when he was gardening, or shingling a roof, or building a fence or a garage or a barn, he asked me to be with him. He used the occasions to talk to me about engineering matters. He also posed practical problems in math. For example, he taught me the usefulness of first making a ballpark estimate of the answer before making a precise calculation.

For a year or two, Father was employed by the Washington State Highway Department. Then he obtained a Civil Service position with the Tacoma Department of Light and Water, where he worked for the rest of his life.

Some of my father's most important and most satisfying employment was in connection with hydroelectric plants built by the City of Tacoma. Soon after he was hired, he was sent to the site of the future Cushman Dam on the Skokomish River. There he supervised obtaining the necessary drill cores to show that the rock at and around the base of the proposed dam were sufficiently solid to warrant construction. He was an assistant in the design of the dam, which was of a fairly unique "control angle" archetype. He also worked on the design of the powerhouse and, ultimately, on the design of the transmission line to Tacoma. This included a mile-long span over the Narrows near Tacoma. Later, during construction, he was the resident engineer on the powerhouse. In 1924, during the construction, I spent a week with him at the site. I went with him down into the "glory hole" and watched while concrete was poured and steel beams were being riveted. It was actually a fairly dangerous spot and not a good place for an 11-year-old boy, but I counted it as a valuable experience.

My father provided other experiences designed to interest me in engineering. In Tacoma, I accompanied him to the office and practiced on the electrical calculator. On one occasion, he brought home a transit. The transit included what amounted to a telescope. We used it to look at the star Polaris and at other heavenly bodies. My father also taught me something about surveying. When I reached the age of 14, he managed to get me a part-time summer job with a private surveyor. I served as a chainman, rodman, and bushwhacker. We surveyed accident scenes, laid out subdivisions, determined the boundary lines between neighbors, and staked out mining claims. The surveying experience later enabled me to pass a civil service examination as an assistant surveyor for the City of Tacoma.

My parents' influence on my early education was supplemented by the influence of my peers. I was fortunate that some of them were children of college graduates. My interaction with two sons of W. W. Durham was particularly constructive.

Durham was trained as an architect, and his son Robert was ultimately a leading Seattle architect. His son Milton became a cancer surgeon and served on the Board of Regents of Washington State University.

One of our memorable joint ventures was to create a museum. It came to contain innumerable biological specimens, such as butterflies. It also had an extensive collection of birds' nests, complete with eggs. I was chief procurer of the nests, and I obtained many rare specimens. Some of the procurement activities included climbing tall trees. On one occasion, I captured an owl in its home in a hollow tree. On another occasion, I helped capture a crow. I would spot a crow's nest high in a tree and would climb up to it. If there were baby crows in the nest, the crows would come darting around, making a tremendous racket. I would have along my trusty slingshot, and, on one occasion, my colleagues on the ground captured a crow that I had hit and stunned. On still another occasion, I was not so successful. I spotted a big nest that was completely enclosed except for an entry hole on the side. I reached into the hole and was promptly attacked by a flying squirrel. The animal took a good bite of my hand, which I quickly withdrew from the hole, bringing with it the squirrel, which instantly released its grip and went sailing gracefully out of sight.

There were many other activities that involved different playmates. We built a small house that had two rooms and a fireplace.

The fireplace functioned perfectly. The lower portion was made of brick, properly mortared together. The fireplace had a chimney made of concrete. As I think back on it, that fireplace had a very good design—a worthy engineering accomplishment for a 12-year-old.

Another activity was a by-product of my father's predilection for having a cow on the place. The family owned irrigated land at Grandview in the Yakima Valley. Father built barns so that he could ship part of the hay crop to Tacoma for our cow and to have some to sell to some of the neighbors. A carload of hay weighed about 15 tons, consisting of 225 bales weighing between 120 pounds and 140 pounds each. The bales had dimensions of four feet long by two feet wide by 15 inches thick. The hay did not completely fill the barn, so there was maneuvering room to move the bales around. I would line up one or more confederates and proceed with a prodigious rearrangement of the bales to form a complex tunnel system. This was done at the time when I was 11 to 13 years old and rather small for my age. Tossing around all those heavy bales was no mean feat, and it involved the expenditure of a tremendous amount of energy in the course of several weeks.

Summer was time for play, work, and adventure. I got my full share of cherries, both from the trees at home and from trees elsewhere in the neighborhood. I earned money picking straw-berries and raspberries in the nearby Puyallup Valley. The main line of the Northern Pacific Railroad ran within about a half mile of home. The railroad yards were only two miles away. There, long freight trains would be assembled, trains destined to go to Auburn and thence across the Cascade Range, heading for St. Paul, Minnesota and the East. Leaving the yards, the long trains accelerated very slowly. Thus, when they passed fairly close, it was possible to catch a ride. The first rides my friends and I took were short, but later rides went on for some miles. We hitch-hiked on the highway to get back home.

One summer day when I was 15, a companion and I decided to venture farther. Our goal was no less than Grandview (eastern Washington), 250 miles away. There we knew Mr. Lyng, who had a farm and who sharecropped my parents' land. We were clad in the flimsiest of summer clothing. By the time the train reached high elevations in the Cascade Range, it was midnight and bitterly cold. We were in an open gondola car. Somehow we endured the cold and were rewarded when we finally reached Grandview. The alfalfa was in bloom, and its perfume was everywhere. We found some work picking plums. After about a week, we rode the freight back home.

Another adventure occurred during the summer when I was 16. Gene Stoll and I learned that construction jobs were to be had in the building of a second dam on the Skokomish River. We decided to go there by hitchhiking, which we did. We were hired to muck rock in the excavation that was to be the site of the concrete dam. This was the "glory hole" in its purest form. The river flowed in a leaky flume above us. The rocks that were to be mucked had been loosened by dynamiting. The resultant boulders came in all sizes and shapes. Many were sharp and jagged and heavy. The task of handling them required maturity and a strong back. I had neither, and by the time I had labored for an hour, my hands were cut and my back was sore. At the end of the day, the boss was merciful. He told me quietly that the job was not for me. On a number of occasions earlier, my mother had quoted, "He who will not use his head must use his back." The one day's experience provided a vivid illustration of the advisability of using one's head.

In October of 1928 or 1929, I had an adventure that could have been lethal. I had visited at the home of Richard Smith. When I got up from a chair to leave, the chair came with me. It seemed that Mrs. Smith had recently varnished the chair, and she thought that the varnish was dry. When I was able to disengage from the chair, I noticed that my pants (my good school pants) were discolored. When I arrived home, my mother was shocked by the sight of them. She told me to go out to the garage to the Model-T Ford and to drain some gasoline from its tank so she could dry-clean my pants. The garage had no light and a dirt floor. On many occasions, when the oil in the car had been changed, the spent oil had been allowed to drain into the dirt below the car. The petcock from which gasoline could be drained

from the Ford was below the middle of the car. Locating the petcock was difficult in the pitch darkness. I finally located the petcock by feel and turned it. Nothing happened, so I lit a match to
size up the situation. Just then came a sudden spurt of gasoline
followed by a muffled explosion. Instantly the region under the
car was aflame. I lost no time departing that scene, beating out
some flames in my clothing.

The car and the garage were a total loss. That week was Fire
Prevention Week in Tacoma, and the incident made a good news
story. My father was named as the party responsible, and he was
described as having lit a match to see how much gasoline was in
the tank. In spite of the notoriety and the loss of car and garage,
my father said not one word of rebuke or criticism to me.

In about 1928, the Light Department decided to build an
additional power plant on the Skokomish River downstream
from the Cushman Dam. The project involved a diversion dam
on the river, a tunnel to conduct the water to a hill overlooking
Hood Canal, and penstocks (large pipes) to bring the water down
to a power plant at sea level. Father designed and produced drawings for the majority of the blueprints used on the job. He was
up-to-date in his designs, often going to the library to supple-
ment his knowledge base. Those power plants were, in effect, an
endowment for the City of Tacoma. Their cost, which was nominal, has long since been amortized, and the water and the electricity continue to flow.

In the autumn of 1929, the City of Tacoma held civil service examinations to recruit the engineering staff necessary to supervise the construction of that second power plant utilizing the water of the Skokomish River. Among the posts to be filled were those of assistant surveyors. The minimum age was 18, but I was only 16 at the time. The examination rating was based on two parts, a written portion and an accounting of past experience. I had had some experience, which was not minimized in the write-up. My brother, who was experienced in surveying, coached me about the written part. My age was listed as 18. A passing grade was 75 or better, and I squeaked by with a grade of 75. In late January, 1930, I was hired as an assistant surveyor and was sent to the engineers' construction camp near Hood Canal and the village of Potlatch, Washington. I was provided with a room and the fabulously good food of a construction camp in addition to a salary of $110 a month. Converted to present dollars, that salary amounted to roughly $3,000 a month. Being naturally frugal, I saved virtually all that I earned and later used the money to pay for all of my first year in college and part of the second year.

When I arrived at the construction camp, I was assigned to assist a Mr. Cechi in providing surveying information for the steelworkers. We had to read the blueprints and make some trigonometric calculations. Because I had had trigonometry in high school, I was able to help Mr. Cechi, who was not well versed in the subject. We worked together for about four weeks.

At that point, Mr. Cechi went to Seattle one weekend, got roaring drunk, and was thrown in jail. The next Monday morning when I reported for work, the chief engineer said, "Abelson, go up on that hill and line in those pipes."

I shouldered the transit and proceeded up the hill. Because I had no assistant, I had to call on steelworkers to hold the rod or plumb bob. I soon observed that they were inclined to cheat on

The surveyor in 1930, standing on the penstocks that
would bring the water down to the power plant.

me to expedite their jobs. Although my upbringing was completely absent of profanity, I was soon out cursing the steelworkers. After that, we got along fine.

My relationship with the steelworkers, though, was disturbed on one other occasion. At about four places on the hill, there were anchors for the pipe, and at one of them the slope changed. I calculated the elevation for the next section of pipe and, when I did so and surveyed in the pipe, the rivet holes did not match as they should have. There was a confrontation, but I was adamant. Grudgingly, the steelworkers placed the pipe where I had dictated. That evening in my room, I grew troubled about the matter. I studied the blueprints and puzzled about the problem until it suddenly occurred to me that I had used the sine of the angle in my calculations when I should have used the tangent. By then it was dusk, and a light rain was falling. I made a roundabout trip through the brush to the penstocks. In the semidarkness, I used jacks to move that five-ton pipe to where it belonged. The next morning, the steelworkers were a little surprised to find that the rivet holes were perfectly aligned, but not a word was said to me (and, of course, I said nothing to anyone). Thereafter, everything went smoothly. At the conclusion of the job, the grizzled old boss steelworker said to me, "Young man, you have a great future ahead of you."

This story was one of Phil's favorites. I think the significance of it for him must have been that mental superiority and the leadership

role that comes with it carry with them more force than the senior-
ity and physical superiority that he clearly did not have, which was a
remarkable lesson for a 16-year-old to learn.

A ll in all, my pre-college experiences were more varied and
enriching than those of most young men. Thus, when I
entered Washington State College in the fall of 1930 at the age of
17, I was immature in some aspects but tougher and more hard-
ened than most young men of my age. Most of all, I knew I was
ready for higher education.

When the time came for me to go to Pullman, my brother
Harold accompanied me, even though he was five years older.
Thereafter, we were good friends and companions. Earlier, the
age gap had been a barrier, and I have only a few memories of him
during the 1920s in Tacoma. While he was growing up, his friends
were not an impressive lot. None of them ever went to college,
and none of their parents had been college
graduates. Harold's friends tended to be
troublemakers in grade school, and most
of them did not finish high school.
Harold's grades were not very good,
although he finished high school with his
age group. After graduating at 18, he
obtained employment as an assistant surveyor for the City of Tacoma. From 1926
to 1930, he was a "good-time Charlie." He

Phil at age 17.

owned a car and was out on the town many evenings. I do recall one incident that surprised me at the time. He had visited friends who had two small babies. He told me about it, and he spoke warmly, almost lovingly, about the little ones.

In early September, 1930, Harold and I made the trip to Pullman with David Hopkins, driven there by David's father. We took up residence together in Stimson Hall, one of the college dormitories. Our association lasted until the Christmas break, when Dave pledged Theta Chi. Each of the three of us was a misfit at Stimson Hall. We did not respect the tone or spirit of the place.

After the first semester, Harold and I moved to a boarding house at 405 Campus Avenue. Later that semester, he pledged Sigma Nu. During the time we roomed together, we became warm friends.

———————————

It is in this context that I relate a story Phil told me around 1987 while we were taking a walk in Pasadena: Harold and Phil had driven one night to Lewiston, Idaho, 20 miles from Pullman. Idaho was a destination for Washington State students for a number of reasons. First, the legal age for drinking was 18 instead of 21, but more profoundly, Idaho had—really still has—a frontier feeling. Idaho is wilder than Washington, and it is wilder in Lewiston than it is in Moscow (home of the University of Idaho), which is just seven miles from Pullman. It is a hazardous drive to get to Lewiston. After driving across the wheat fields for 15 miles, you get to the canyon of the Snake River and the road tortuously switches back repeatedly down the wall of the canyon for several miles until you get to the valley and Clarkston, Washington.

Then you drive across the bridge over the Snake River into Lewiston. The trip home is even more hazardous.

After some unspecified activities, it was very late at night and Harold and Phil were walking along a street in Lewiston. Harold stopped to pee in the street, and he was observed doing so by a policeman. Both Harold and Phil ended up in the Lewiston jail. It was an active night at the jail. There had been a roundup of prostitutes from the local brothel, which, together with the usual inebriated occupants of the jail, made it a very noisy place. The madam of the brothel visited the jail, seeking to retrieve her employees. Phil did not say whether she was successful in this, but she did spot Harold and Phil, and she persuaded the jailer to release them. Left unsaid in this story was whom she had recognized. Presumably it was my father, Harold. It is only the young that can come home after a night like this and continue to study chemistry, but that is probably what Phil did.

I was asked to join a number of fraternities, but I sized up the situation in this way: First of all, if I were to join a fraternity, I would likely have to put up with some hazing. Secondly, I would probably be expected to tutor some of the denser fraternity brothers and to spend much of my time and energy on the various fraternity activities. I had it in mind that I was going to study, I was going to get good grades, and I was going to complete the work toward a bachelor's degree as soon as possible.

When I first registered at the college, I chose chemical engineering as my major. The choice reflected the warm experience I had had in chemistry in one semester in high school. The engineering part represented a compromise designed to move toward the wishes of my father. He did not bring overt pressure on me to major in civil engineering, but I sensed that he hoped that I would do so. I had concluded, however, that in order to be a top civil engineer, one also had to be a good politician. That is, obtaining the authorization to take on major projects requires significant negotiation, and the choice of the top engineer might or might not be made only on the basis of the sterling technical qualities of the engineers vying for the job. I felt that my father was an excellent engineer who might well have had greater success in his profession if he had had the right background and connections. I had the impression that scientists who sought after knowledge would be judged by their achievements and that politics would not have a large role. Later I learned that, in the real world, politics is everywhere.

During my freshman year, I took a number of engineering courses. The professors of those courses were not inspiring, and the content was not particularly interesting. I found I had little talent for mechanical drawing or for visualizing complex structures in three dimensions. In contrast, I enjoyed the first year of college chemistry, which was taught enthusiastically by Julian Culbertson. I especially enjoyed the laboratory work. Ahead of each lab session, I studied the manual and planned my activities to maximize my efficiency. I went to the lab early and stayed late.

Chemistry and a well-taught course in English composition were the bright spots in an otherwise rather drab existence. At

Stimson Hall, the day began at 6:00 A.M. Breakfast at the Commons (not very appetizing) was served at 6:30, and an obligatory Reserve Officers Training Corps session (in uniform) began every morning at 7:00. There followed classes, more Commons, and study until 11:00 P.M. On the weekends, there was often attendance at an athletic event, but mainly there was more study.

Toward the end of the freshman year, my brother Harold told me of an opportunity to get college credit for the experience I had had in surveying. To obtain it, I would have to pass an examination in some course work that he had been taking. He coached me on what was likely to be covered in the exam. Thus prepared, I successfully passed the test. Later, the professor told Harold that I would have received an A if I had been enrolled in the course, but since I had merely taken the exam, he could only give me a B.

During the following summer, I reflected on the extra credit I had received for the surveying course and on some good grades I had earned in chemistry and calculus. I concluded that it would make sense for me to switch my major to chemistry and thereby create the option of graduating from college in three years rather than four. I studied the college catalog for requirements to graduate in chemistry and concluded that finishing early would be feasible if I were to master the first semester of German that summer. I never truly mastered German, but I learned enough to enable me to skip the first course.

My sophomore year was marvelous. I took a heavy load of courses in mathematics, chemistry, and physics. I was especially intrigued by organic chemistry, which I still regard as one of the great triumphs of the human mind. Courses in qualitative and quantitative analysis were not particularly exciting. However, with my established methods of preparation for lab work, I was able to complete the unknowns in quantitative analysis before the semester was half over. The professor was pleased, and he rewarded me by giving me extra work to do, which I cheerfully went about accomplishing. I found all my courses interesting, and I studied faithfully. The heavy load did not burden me. I was not a perfectionist. I aimed for an A with the belief that most of the time that is what I would achieve. Sometimes I might miss a little and get a B+, which would then be recorded as a B.

At the end of my sophomore year, I realized that if I went to summer school, I could complete my bachelor's degree in one more year with credits to spare. To accomplish this, I took courses in biochemistry, complex variables, and electrochemical research.

That autumn, I laid out another heavy schedule of study—heavy enough that I had to obtain approval from Dean C. C. Todd. He asked me a pointed question, one that I was neither experienced enough nor informed enough to appreciate fully. He asked, "What's your hurry?" I was not really aware of the deep troubles that the nation was then enduring. I did not realize the magnitude of the Great Depression or the way in which it was affecting opportunities for young chemists. Later I was to witness at close range some of the misery that many people were experiencing.

Harold and I were shielded from the Depression in two ways. We were studying at a campus far from the big-city slums, and my father had steady employment throughout the hard times. My parents were frugal people and, in proportion to their expenditures, were well off. In terms of 2003 dollars, my father's salary was $100,000 or more. There was also a modest income from the farm in the Yakima Valley. The cow provided milk, some of which was sold to neighbors. Expenses were minimal. My parents had their food, clothing, and shelter at minimum cost. They did not spend money on luxuries.

I have often considered the monetary and energy expenditures of my parents in the context of life in Tacoma in the era of the 1920s and 1930s. Home heating was with wood. There was a car, but it was operated only occasionally for short trips. Father rode the streetcar (and later the bus) to work. Electricity consumption was nominal. Their total annual energy consumption was probably one-tenth or less than that of the average family of today. In any generation, there are anxieties and problems, both real and imagined. It is obvious to me that there is more anxiety and discontent today than there was then.

———————————

The most important thing that happened to Phil in this period is told in his favorite and most heartfelt story:

> One day, outside the Chemistry Building, I saw a girl walking across the campus. She walked erect with a brisk and purposeful stride and she was smiling. I didn't know her, but I made inquiries, and I found that she was in a beginning chemistry class. Her professor told me who she was. That girl was Neva.

During my last year as an undergraduate, I took courses in physics and physical chemistry, as well as some in non-science areas that were required for graduation. One was in public speaking. I had not had occasion earlier to make a formal oral presentation. When I spoke before the class, I was pleased to note that my remarks were well received. I had a similar experience in a senior seminar in chemistry.

After the first semester of my senior year, I was in a position to relax a little in my studies. Some of the courses were neither extremely interesting nor particularly demanding. Also, Harold and I had a car at Pullman, which had been provided by our parents. Earlier, we had returned to Tacoma from Pullman riding the freight trains, but our parents much preferred that we come home by car.

2

Riding the Rails

In the last semester of my senior year, I had taken a course in pharmacy and had learned how to make various consumer products, including shaving cream. I had told my brother about what I knew, and he, in turn, informed a fraternity brother named Dan Dech. The upshot was that, immediately after graduation in June of 1933, I went to Spokane with Dech, and we cooked up batches of shaving cream, which he peddled.

I did not tarry long in Spokane but made my way home to Tacoma. Home was very pleasant, but I was (and still am) a person who likes action. In the Depression year of 1933, there were no jobs in Tacoma, so I considered taking a trip to visit the world's fair in Chicago (the Century of Progress Exhibition of 1933–1934). Such a journey could include a visit to Neva in Pullman, too.

During my senior year, I had stayed in a house shared by a rural school superintendent named Waggoner, whose brother was a physician in Chicago. In that year, the Chicago world's fair was much in the news as a glamorous and important event. Waggoner and I had conversations about the fair, and he told me that, if I wished to go there, he would ask his brother to provide me lodging. The arrangement was made.

In early July, I bought a knapsack that would hold a good suit of clothes and other spare minor garments. That evening, I packed my things and then hopped a freight train headed east. Freight trains in the Northwest in those days followed a leisurely course. They stopped at numerous junction points, where some cars were removed, other cars were added, and crews were changed. In two days, I was in Pullman. After a day's visit with Neva, I went to Spokane, where I hopped a freight train destined for St. Paul, Minnesota. All the cars on the train except one were loaded and their doors were shut. Thus, all the hoboes congregated in the one empty boxcar. There were about eighty of them, and most of them had not bathed in quite a while. Many of the hoboes had removed their shoes.

Fortunately, at the next junction point, additional empty boxcars were added, along with some empty gondola cars. The weather was pleasant and the scenery was great. I stayed with the train, stopping when it did and, whenever possible, buying some simple food or bathing and shaving. Staying with the train as I did

Hopping aboard a freight car on the fly was
dangerous and many people got hurt doing it.

was not conducive to sleep. The cars jumped and swayed, and
their hard floors did not make for a comfortable bed. Thus, on
the evening when we arrived in St. Paul, I was tired and sleepy,
but I was determined to press on to Chicago. From conversations
with other travelers, I learned that a daily express freight would
be leaving at about 8:00 P.M. for Chicago. It would make the trip

in about nine hours. There would be no empty cars on the train. That meant that I would have to ride atop one of the boxcars or cling to one of the ladders that were attached to either end of each car.

It was a hot summer night with frequent showers. Rather than exposing myself completely to the driving rain by riding on top of a car, I chose to cling to the rungs of a ladder. Along about 1:00 A.M., I noted that a week's cumulative lack of sleep was

"I chose to cling to the rungs of a ladder."

catching up with me. I hooked my arms in a rung of the ladder in such a way that, if I were to doze off and relax, my arms would give me warning before I fell beneath the wheels of the train. It was fortunate that I had taken that precaution, because I did momentarily fall asleep, and my locked arms saved me. That experience gave me such a jolt of adrenaline that I was able to stay awake for the remainder of the journey to Chicago.

On arriving in Chicago, I found a place to shave, clean up, and change into my good suit. I found my way to Dr. Wagoner's combined residence and office, where I was received kindly. I slept there each night, but I had my meals elsewhere. During the following week, I attended the world's fair a number of times, and I also visited other points of interest, including the Field Museum. I rode the streetcars and the El. On one occasion, I visited briefly an all-night theater on skid row (then near State Street) where, for a dime, people could have shelter for the night. There was a marked contrast between those who could afford the admission fee to the fair and those others on skid row.

At the end of a week in Chicago, my funds were almost depleted, so it was time to move on. I considered going farther east, but I decided instead to return to Tacoma via Los Angeles. The route would take me through the Dust Bowl, and I was to encounter a harsher side of America than when I traveled east on the northern route. The westward route would include Kansas City, Missouri; Wichita, Kansas; El Reno, Oklahoma; back to

Wichita; Liberal, Kansas; Tucumcari, New Mexico; El Paso, Texas; Yuma, Arizona; Los Angeles, Bakersfield, Sacramento, and Weed, California; Bend, Oregon; Pasco and Pullman, Washington; and, finally, Tacoma.

Travel to Wichita proceeded smoothly. The trip took about two days. There were no empty boxcars, so I climbed to the top of a car and lay on the catwalk. On a pleasant sunny day, the ride was relaxing. The car swayed gently from side to side. Since I have never sleepwalked or fallen out of bed, I felt perfectly secure in dozing off to sleep.

At Wichita, I hopped a freight that took me to a big junction point at El Reno, Oklahoma. There I encountered the first of a series of brutalities. About 100 travelers attempted to hop a freight train headed west. As the train began to pick up speed, a crew of railroad deputies ("dicks"), armed with clubs, chased the travelers or bludgeoned them off the train. I noted what was going on and decided to leave El Reno as rapidly as possible. It so happened that I was standing on the opposite side of the tracks from the passenger station when a train stopped briefly to pick up and discharge passengers. In those days, a baggage car was always next to the locomotive. It had a platform where one could stand. The space was known among railroad people and hoboes as "blind baggage." I quickly boarded the train and ensconced myself in blind baggage. We left El Reno at about 8:00 P.M. and went nonstop to Wichita, Kansas. The experience was not ideal. The locomotive burned fuel

"A burly detective hit me in the eye as I ran for a train."

oil, but rather inefficiently. A certain fraction of the oil and soot landed on me as I rode in blind baggage.

I had been told by fellow travelers that railroad detectives awaited passenger trains coming into major stations and that it would be advisable to leave the train before it reached the station. As we approached Wichita and the train slowed, I attempted to disembark. However, my knapsack limited my maneuverability. The moment I hit the ground, I was accosted by a detective. He shined a flashlight on me and asked, "Are you a nigger?" I don't know what would have ensued if he had determined that I was. He did no violence to me, but he conducted me directly to the Wichita jail. There I was fingerprinted and photographed, and then I was placed in a large cell with about 30 other men. The cell was completely barren, without chairs, and it had a concrete floor. There was no water closet, only a hole in the floor about four inches in diameter that was meant to serve as a not-so-private privy. It was a Saturday night, so many of the occupants of the cell were there because they had been obnoxiously drunk in public. Next to our cell, and well within earshot, was a comparable facility for women. That evening, the Wichita police had raided the red-light district, where they had harvested a bumper crop. The women were very unhappy about their circumstance, and they were determined to tell the world about it. They found considerable sympathy among those in our cell. During much of the night, the air was filled with ribald shouts.

The next morning, we were fed an inedible breakfast, and I was then conducted to a judge who told me he was going to let me go, but that if I were caught again in Wichita, I would be sentenced to "spend six months on the bean farm." I located a spot some distance from the center of the city where I could hop a freight train, and thus I managed to avoid the bean farm.

Years later, when I had to fill out forms to obtain a security clearance, one of the questions was, "Have you ever been in jail?" I gulped, but I answered the question in the affirmative, noting that it was for "vagrancy in Wichita." I suspect that someone must have been a little shocked that this respectable Ph.D. had been jailed, but there was no mention of it to me.[1]

The continuation of the journey westward took me through part of the Dust Bowl. Evidence of drought damage was particularly striking around Liberal, Kansas. The fields were completely barren. Nowhere was there any green living thing to be seen. The soil had been blown about, and a few dried tumbleweeds were the only evidence that any vegetation had ever grown there.

The next stop was in Tucumcari, New Mexico. This was a small town, but it was a major junction point on the railroad. Once again, the railroad police were much in evidence. They were attempting to discourage further travel toward El Paso, Texas and points west.

Sometimes the engineer would back the train up the track before moving past the station so that it could get up speed before it came past the place where the nonpaying riders would usually try to get aboard. Thus, the train was moving fairly fast when I moved to hop on. A burly detective hit me in the eye as I ran for the train, causing a big shiner that lasted for more than a week. Nevertheless, I managed to catch the train on the fly. The

---

[1] Using the Freedom of Information Act I obtained Phil's FBI file—all 90 pages. He did in fact admit this arrest and it is just about all they found. He was actually investigated three times. This was in 1947. Then, in 1957, J. Edgar Hoover took it upon himself to investigate everyone who had anything to do with the Manhattan project (or at least that is my interpretation). Then, in 1960, President Eisenhower asked for a security clearance because Phil was being nominated as an advisor to the Atomic Energy Commission (AEC).

trip to El Paso and then to Yuma, Arizona, proceeded without further incidence.

In my travels, I did not seek companionship. However, when I needed directions or other information, I did not hesitate to mingle with other travelers. Thus, as we approached California, I talked with others who had heard tales about the rough treatment that hoboes were encountering there. The closer we came to the state, the more intense the warnings became. Specifically, we were told that Los Angeles was building a new Lincoln Heights jail. The laborers constructing the jail were hoboes, who, having been caught, had been sentenced to work for some months on the construction site.

Although I was apprehensive, I was nevertheless determined to continue my journey to Los Angeles. But we were only about 30 miles within California when the freight train came to a halt in the desert. A crew of railroad detectives combed the train and gathered me and the 70 other travelers into a small area. We were then required to relinquish all of our valuables, including our money, except for one dollar. Each of us was then given a non-redeemable passenger tickets to travel a distance corresponding to the amount of money taken. It was sad to see some of the old men cry, for they had no place to go, and the money taken from them, in some cases, represented the last of their life savings. I was not affected that much, because I only had 75 cents to begin with. Furthermore, I had a home to go to, if I could avoid construction work on the Lincoln Heights jail.

As we approached Los Angeles, the train slowed about 20 miles from the city center. I had been informed that the spot was a good one at which to disembark and that I might purchase a ticket to ride into the city on an interurban train. Accordingly, I left the freight train and managed to shave, clean up, and change into my suit. I then paid 25 cents to ride in style into Los Angeles. It was late in the day when I arrived, and there ensued a nervous moment. I was dressed respectably, but I had a knapsack on my back and a big black eye. I walked along and came to a street corner. Across the road was a policeman. He looked me over searchingly, started to make a move in my direction, but then, at the last moment, changed his mind and did not accost me. I proceeded to move sedately out of his sight. It seemed clear to me, however, that I had better find shelter for the night. I did so at a rescue mission. In those days, there was a string of missions up and down the West Coast. The down-and-out were given a meal, were expected to listen to a religious service, and were then given a place to sleep for the night. The food was palatable, the service was not too lengthy, and I had a good night's sleep.

Very early the next morning, I found my way to a major highway, where I was fortunate to quickly hitch a ride with a young man who was driving to Sacramento via Bakersfield. We had a pleasant conversation, and the trip was fast. At Sacramento, I located the yards of the Western Pacific to catch a train proceeding to Weed in northeastern California, which was the junction point to the Great Northern spur between Weed and

Pasco, Washington. I arrived in Weed late in the day after a long day's travel from Los Angeles. I had not eaten all day, and I was hungry. I bought some navy beans, found an old coffee can, built a fire, and ultimately had a salt-free dinner of half-cooked beans. Soon I was aboard a fast freight that stopped only briefly at Bend, Oregon, and I arrived in Pasco the next morning. By then I was in familiar terrain. I visited Neva briefly in Pullman, where I learned the good news that I had been appointed to be a teaching assistant in physics for the coming academic year. The journey home to Tacoma was uneventful.

I would not recommend to others that they have the kind of adventures that I had during my five-week, 7500-mile trip. For me, however, it was a useful experience. Before the trip, I had lived a privileged and sheltered life among caring people, both at home and in schools and college. On my trip to Chicago and back, I saw quite a bit of life in the raw during the time of the Great Depression. The travelers I encountered were generally kind people. I noted a number of homeless families, but I never heard of women being molested. The only cruelty and meanness that I met with on my trip was on the part of petty officials.

Later, I could appreciate a statement that Ross Gunn often made: "The principal value of money is to insulate you from the sons of bitches of the world." Perhaps the principal value of the experience for me was as a yardstick. After one comes through such an experience, other tight situations do not cause one to lose his cool.

3

A Start in Physics

The invitation to become a teaching assistant in physics was highly welcome. I had not tried to obtain a graduate fellowship in chemistry at Washington State or elsewhere. In my last undergraduate year, I had taken upper-division courses in physics, including "Kinetic Theory of Gases." These courses were taught by Paul Anderson, who was an enthusiastic, charismatic teacher. During my sophomore year (1931) I had made a policy decision to live a life of learning. Going for a master's degree in physics would broaden my base of knowledge and would prepare me for additional opportunities. The presence of Neva in Pullman was also an important factor.

The two years that followed were largely devoted to studies, teaching, and research. My course work included some upper-division courses and some at the graduate level. I taught tutorial

Professor Paul Anderson from Washington State University,
Department of Physics.

sections in first-year physics, covering mechanics, sound, electricity and magnetism, and optics. Professor Anderson was, at that time, conducting research on contact potentials. The work involved the use of electron streams in a high vacuum with measurements of the potentials of clean surfaces. The experimental apparatus was built of Pyrex glass, and the experimenter created

it by blowing the glass. Even after much practice, I was undistin-
guished as a glassblower. After some trauma, I did manage to
make a usable, fairly complex piece of equipment, and, in due
course, I measured contact potentials of various concentrations
of barium amalgams. The results formed the basis of a thesis,
but not much more.

During the second year of my assistantship (for which I
received $350 per annum), I took two graduate courses that I
found especially enjoyable. Both courses were taught by S.
Towne Stephenson, who had recently come to Pullman after
earning a doctorate at Yale. The courses were "Introduction to
Theoretical Physics" and "Introduction to Modern Physics." The
latter course was based on a text by Floyd Richtmyer. It dealt
with such matters as the Bohr atom and quantum theory. As an
assignment for library study, I read and reported on an article by
Ernest Lawrence describing the cyclotron. It was an exciting
paper, and I was convinced that nuclear physics was a field with a
future.

I consulted with Anderson and Stephenson, and both
encouraged me to apply for a teaching assistantship at Berkeley.
Both wrote letters on my behalf. I suspected that Stephenson's
letter might have been particularly effective. Lawrence had been
at Yale before going to Berkeley, and Stephenson and Lawrence

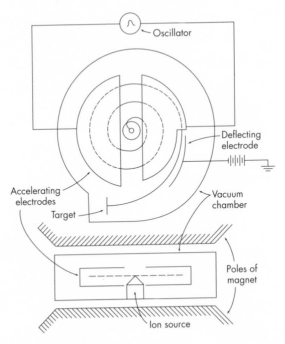

The cyclotron has three basic parts: a large magnet, and a vacuum chamber enclosing two D-shaped electrodes between the poles of the magnet. The electrodes are alternately charged by an oscillator. Positively charged particles (e.g., protons or deuterons) are introduced in the center between the electrodes and are accelerated toward the negative pole. In a magnetic field, a charged particle moves in a circular path whose radius depends on the velocity of the particle and the magnitude of the magnetic field. The oscillator is tuned so that, when the particle returns to the gap between the electrodes, the polarity of the field is changed and the particle is again accelerated by the electric field. In this way, the particle spirals outward, gaining energy in each pass through the electric field. Thus, the energy of the particle depends on the diameter and strength of the magnet. To study the nucleus requires perturbing its structure via bombardment with high-energy particles. Phil knew that those who could generate particles with the highest energies would eventually make important discoveries.

had many friends in common. In any event, I was awarded a teaching assistantship ($600 per year), and I was the only person that year from out of state to be so favored.

———————————

That Anderson and Stephenson encouraged Phil to go to Berkeley instead of influencing him (likely their best student) to stay at Pullman was perhaps the most important benefit of Phil's education at Washington State. This unselfish promotion of a student is, I think, a story that is very typical of the land-grant colleges and universities in our country, and it helps to explain why so many of our great scientists have come out of that system.

4

With Lawrence at Berkeley: The Discovery of Nuclear Fission

I arrived in Berkeley in August 1935, quickly found a place with room and board, and immediately proceeded to Lawrence's Radiation Laboratory. He was there, and, without delay, he directed me to paint the cyclotron magnet. The vacuum chamber of the cyclotron was being repaired. The 80-ton magnet was black, and he wanted it painted a battleship gray. I proceeded about that business and was soon joined by Lawrence himself. During the ensuing days, I was assigned to do some odd jobs, but soon I was assigned to heavy duty as part of the cyclotron crew. At that time, the machine was scheduled to operate for 15 hours a day, seven days a week. The particles accelerated by the cyclotron were used to irradiate elements directly or to generate neutrons that could be used to produce artificial isotopes (usually

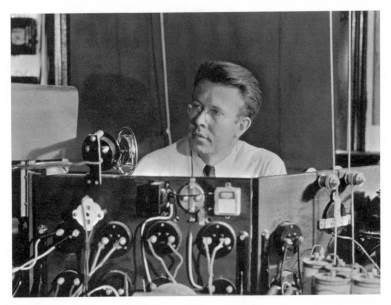

Ernest Lawrence at the controls of the 37" cyclotron in 1938 (photo from
Lawrence Radiation Lab)

radioactive ones). Lawrence was constantly pushing to increase
the beam current and the energy of the particles.

Lawrence conceived of the idea for the cyclotron in 1929,
shortly after he arrived at Berkeley from Yale at the age of 28. The
first instrument, built in 1931, was only 4.5 inches in diameter, and
the voltage between the D-shaped electrodes was less than 1000
volts, but it produced protons with energies of 80,000 electron
volts. By 1932, energies of 1,000,000 electron volts were being
produced by a machine with a diameter of 11 inches. By the time
Phil arrived at Berkeley, the workhorse cyclotron was 27 inches in
diameter, and it produced energies of 5,000,000 electron volts

The 27-inch cyclotron in Lawrence's Radiation Laboratory could produce energies of 5 MeV.

(5 MeV). A 37-inch cyclotron and a 60-inch cyclotron were built while he was there. The magnet of the latter instrument weighed almost 200 tons.

The operating schedule for the cyclotron was divided into three shifts: roughly 8 A.M. to 1 P.M., 1 P.M. to 6 P.M., and 6 P.M. to 11 P.M. That was only nominal, though, because leaks often developed, or an internal filament used to ionize deuterium would need to be changed, or the vacuum chamber would have to be taken apart. When such emergencies arose, all hands were supposed to respond. In 1935 and 1936, I was one of the few graduate students working in the lab. Most of the others were postdocs. They were assigned three shifts per week, while I was assigned six shifts plus emergency duty. Emergencies were frequent, because the cyclotron chamber had joints that were sealed with beeswax and natural resin called glyptal. To function properly, the chamber vacuum needed to be on the order of 10^{-6} mm Hg. Thus, a tiny leak would make the machine inoperable. We hunted for leaks by exposing suspected regions to the ethane from natural gas. Ethane went through the leak faster than air,

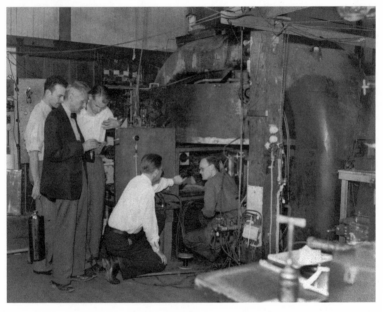

Coaxing the 27" cyclotron to work are F. Kurie, Donald Cooksey, Ed McMillan, Lawrence, and R. Thornton.

and it produced a change in the level of the vacuum that was observable at the control panel.

For the first two years of my time at Berkeley, I spent an average of 40 hours each week on what amounted to menial care of the cyclotron. I was, of course, expected to do other things. As a teaching assistant, I worked as a lab instructor, and I corrected the blue books of examinations taken by classes of 500 elementary physics students. Correcting blue books for Leonard Loeb was a trying adventure. He took the view that students should be given partial credit on a question if they showed some sign of understanding what the problem was all about. In some instances, the 500 students would devise about 50 different ways of not getting the right answer to a question. Apportioning partial credit to the various versions would have taxed Solomon. Even more trying was maintaining consistency, which was especially necessary because the students were given to comparing answers and grades.

At the end of 1936, six months after he had seemed wary of marriage in his birthday letter to his mother, Phil and Neva were married in Tacoma. By this time, Neva had graduated from Washington State and had begun her medical studies at the University of California, San Francisco, across the bay.

Neva and Phil on their wedding day, December 30, 1936, in Tacoma, Washington.

Graduate students were required to take graduate courses and ultimately to take preliminary examinations to prove that they had mastered the content of the courses they had taken. This part of graduate school was something of a torture for me. None of the professors was a good teacher, and none of them exhibited any enthusiasm for meeting with their classes. They provided no judgment of what was interesting or important. I learned little, and I barely squeaked through the prelims.

Phil's particular nemesis in his oral exams must have been Robert Oppenheimer. Oppenheimer was brilliant and corrosive, and he could (and did) make even Lawrence look bad. The oral exam took place only a few months before the awarding of Phil's

Phil with my parents Ruth and Harold on a trip they took to California in 1936.

Ph.D. A Chinese student, Chien-Shiung Wu, who later became famous for her experiment at Columbia University that disproved parity, took her exam in the morning and Phil took his in the afternoon with the same committee that included Oppenheimer and Lawrence. The contrast between the two students was painful. Wu knew theoretical physics and passed easily. Phil passed, but he was convinced that this was only because Lawrence would not allow one of his students to flunk. At home that night, Neva had a celebration dinner waiting, but there was no celebration.

A graduate student in the Radiation Lab was also supposed to do research. Doing that took up the rest of the 100 hours a week that I spent on various scholarly duties. My first participation in research was as a collaborator in a ^{32}P tracer experiment.

This came about on the urging of Ernest Lawrence. In this country, individuals and foundations then and now are far more willing to support research related to medicine than to the physical sciences. Thus, the pathway to bigger and better cyclotrons would come most easily via applications of the machine to biology and medicine. Two professors in the Life Sciences Building at Berkeley wanted to use ^{32}P to trace the rate of incorporation of phosphate into the soft tissues and bones of chickens. I furnished the radioactive phosphate; they administered it to growing chicks and then supplied me with the various chicken parts. I treated them with chemicals to destroy the organic matter, and I measured the radioactivity of aliquots of the resultant phosphate on an electroscope after determining the total amount of phosphate in the sample by standard quantitative techniques. In due course (1936), a paper by Cook, Scott, and Abelson appeared in the *Proceedings of the National Academy of Sciences*. It was no world-beater, although it was one of the first ^{32}P tracer studies conducted in the United States.[1]

One day in early 1936, Lawrence remarked about a paper by Fermi and colleagues in which they had irradiated uranium with neutrons and had produced beta emitters that they believed were transuranic elements.

At this point it is worthwhile to review the developments in physics that related to the important issues in Phil's thesis research. In 1934, following the discovery of artificial radioactivity by Frédéric and Irène Joliot-Curie, Enrico Fermi in Rome had systematically bombarded all of the elements with slow neutrons. With the heavier elements, neutron capture generally resulted in isotopes that were one or two atomic masses heavier. In some cases, these isotopes were radioactive and would decay with the release of one or more electrons, making an element of higher atomic number. These transmuted elements could be identified by precipitation of the radioactive substance with known carrier elements.

---

[1] Phosphate is a component of nucleic acids and many small molecules in the cell, and ^{32}P is still in common use in biochemistry and molecular biology 60 years later.

Irradiation of uranium, the heaviest naturally occurring element, produced radioactive material with several different half-lives, suggesting that a new element with a higher atomic number (called a transuranic element) had been created. In this case, however, there was no carrier available to substantiate this claim. Various precipitations ruled out most of the radiation decay products of uranium, and a tentative claim was made for the discovery of element 93, later called ekarhenium because it was precipitated together with rhenium sulfate. As the periodic table was drawn then, rhenium was just above element 93, so the two elements would be expected to have similar chemical properties. Several groups (including Frédéric and Irène Joliot-Curie in Paris and Otto Hahn, Lise Meitner, and Fritz Strassmann in Berlin) continued to study the products of neutron irradiation of uranium and found a plethora of products with different half-lives. They did not initially challenge Fermi's basic conclusion that a new transuranic element had been created.

In the uranium decay series, electron emission is followed by the emission of alpha particles. The high levels of neutrons available from the cyclotron made it seem possible that irradiation of uranium might lead to detectable alpha particles emitted by the new transuranic element. I irradiated some uranium and separated the transuranic elements following the procedures described by Fermi. Lawrence and I jointly looked for alpha particles, but we found none. My efforts to discover more about the effects of irradiating uranium with neutrons did not stop there. However, the more intense irradiation yielded only more complexity.

When a single radioactive isotope is produced, it decays exponentially with a characteristic half-life. When the intensity is plotted as a function of time on semi-log graph paper, the result is a straight line. When I followed the decay of the irradiated uranium and plotted the results on semi-log graph paper, the result was a curve instead of a straight line, indicating that a complex mixture of decay products had been formed. For a time, I relegated the uranium question to a lower priority, and I turned to such practical matters as passing my prelim exams.

By 1937, my standing in the hierarchy of the Radiation Lab had improved. One day, Donald Cooksey approached me, asking for my help in finding the leaks in a newly designed cyclotron vacuum chamber. This one had an enlarged diameter of 37 inches. It would be able to produce 8-MeV deuterons.

Best of all, though, the vacuum chamber on the new cyclotron would not be sealed with beeswax and resin. Instead, much of the assembly would be welded together and, where necessary, rubber gaskets would be employed. Cooksey had assembled the chamber and had attempted to obtain a good vacuum in it. He had failed, and he concluded that some of the welds were leaking. Ultimately, I found 23 different leaks of varying sizes. It was tedious work because it was only feasible to find the largest leak first, stop it, and then proceed to find the next largest. When the whole deed was done and the new chamber was installed, the cyclotron produced more-energetic beams and the operation of a chamber devoid of resin and beeswax was relatively trouble-free.

By the summer of 1937, demand for tracers from the cyclotron had increased substantially. Operation of the machine was scheduled on a 24-hour basis. I spent many a lonely night on the owl shift, which went from 11 P.M. to 8 A.M. My memory is that I was an excellent operator who made the necessary adjustments to keep the beam constantly at maximum and that there were no breakdowns while I was in charge.

———————

Lawrence clearly expected a superhuman effort from his group. Morale was high, though, because Lawrence had attracted some of the brightest students in America to his laboratory, and, although Lawrence was increasingly absent as Phil's tenure proceeded, Phil received strong support from the older members of the laboratory, particularly Luis Alvarez and Edwin McMillan. The roster of the lab at this time became a pantheon of American physics.

By early 1938, I had completed the required courses and had finished most of the prelims. I had been given a research assistantship, too. The cyclotron was operating more reliably, so I had more freedom to resume research. At that time, each member of the laboratory had to make his own measuring equipment. With some help from others, I became equipped with a

The scientists at the Radiation Lab assembled between the jaws of the magnet for the 60-inch cyclotron, circa 1939. Lawrence is in the middle of the first row. Phil is all the way to the right in the first row, next to Luis Alvarez. Ed McMillan is fourth from the left in the second row.

sensitive electroscope and a Geiger counter and made my own Geiger tubes, determining their proper operating voltages. I had laboratory space in Le Conte Hall. Thus, I had everything necessary to pursue independent research.

What to do, though? There was only limited inspiration or guidance to be had. Ernest Lawrence's main interest and top priority by far was designing and financing machines that could produce higher-energy particles. Most of the research being done at

Luis Alvarez with an ionization
chamber he built, 1938.

the Radiation Lab was directed at the discovery of radioactive
isotopes, and the leading figures in that effort were Jack Living-
good and Glenn Seaborg. Theirs was excellent work but not
inspiring. The one person in the lab who was enthusiastically cre-
ative was Luis Alvarez. He also had time for a graduate student,
and we frequently went to the Student Union nearby to have coffee. I sought his advice, and he encouraged me to resume work
on the neutron irradiation of uranium. I did so, and I found that I
could isolate a three-day radioactivity that had a 2.4-hour daughter product. The chemistry employed to separate the three-day
activity was one that an eka-rhenium element might have.

About that time, Alvarez discovered that electron capture occurred in the decay of an isotope of gallium, leading to the emission of characteristic x rays. These x rays, as well as gamma rays, were produced from the internal conversion of energy. I looked for x rays from the combined three-day parent daughter product. I found the x rays and gamma rays there, too. However, steeped in the Fermi doctrine, I attributed the radiation to the possible characteristic x rays of a transuranic element. Accordingly, I set out to find a method for measuring their wavelength. Alvarez was aware of a fairly recent publication about a sensitive bent-crystal x-ray spectrometer, which I proceeded to build and test. I used it to identify characteristic x rays associated with the decay of ^{64}Cu, ^{67}Ga, ^{80}Br, and a technetium isotope (*Physical Review* **1939**, *56*, 753–757). I was prepared to tackle the x-ray emitter associated with the product of neutron irradiation of uranium. The intensity of the radiation was the limiting factor. My experience with the other x-ray emitters told me that I must expose a large amount of uranium to as many neutrons as possible over a long period of time. However, the financial position of the Radiation Lab at that time was precarious, and I could not expect the Lab to buy the necessary chemicals.

―――――――

Although Lawrence was one of the great money raisers of all time, almost all of the money went to building ever-larger cyclotrons. As a result, about half of the people in his laboratory were volunteers. In fact, Don Cooksey, Lawrence's assistant director, quietly contributed his own money to buy supplies and equipment for the laboratory.

Lawrence expected as much of the volunteers as of the paid staff. One might have thought him a slave driver, but morale in the lab was high. Lawrence was there when he was not traveling and would initiate procedures himself. Once, he nearly killed Phil by walking into the control room of the cyclotron and turning on the high voltage, not seeing Phil working near the rear of the cyclotron. "I was two or three inches away from frying," he reported later.

For Christmas, 1938, my parents sent me $25 to buy a new suit. In early January, 1939, Neva and I crossed the bay by ferry to San Francisco to do the shopping. On our way there, we stopped at Braun, Knecht, and Heiman Chemical Suppliers.[2] We emerged from their shop (the suit money spent) with 10 pounds of yellowcake uranium. Back in Berkeley, I found it to be very impure. Among other things, it contained silicates, which formed gels when the product was acidified. It was only after some effort that the uranium was freed of major impurities.

———————

Meanwhile, during the fall of 1938, Otto Hahn and Fritz Strassmann had carried out an exhaustive series of precipitation experiments on the products of the neutron irradiation of

———————

[2] The store was located at 548 Mission Street.

uranium, three of which they had earlier thought to be isotopes of radium. By this time, their colleague Lise Meitner was no longer in Berlin. She had moved to Stockholm to avoid the persecution of Jews then so actively progressing in Germany. In that series of experiments, Hahn and Strassmann discovered that an 86-minute half-life "radium" isotope precipitated, even crystallized, with barium chloride.

Hahn was a rigorous chemist, and he did a series of beautiful mixing experiments showing, for example, that the known isotopes of radium failed to precipitate when added to the mixture. He was beginning to conclude, by a process of elimination, that the product was actually barium—but how could uranium, atomic number 92, decay to barium, atomic number 56? Hahn was continuously corresponding with Meitner (in Stockholm), who was also puzzled. The final clincher came with the characterization of the beta decay product. If it were a radium isotope, the product should be actinium; if it were a barium isotope, the product should be lanthanum. Lanthanum is separable chemically from actinium. Thus, the reaction is

$$_{92}U + n \rightarrow \ _{56}Ba + \ _{36}Kr$$

On December 21, 1938, Hahn again wrote to Meitner to confirm that the decay product was indeed lanthanum. Meitner did not immediately receive this letter because she had left Stockholm to spend Christmas with family members in a small town near Goteborg. Among them was her nephew Otto Frisch, also a physicist, who had come to Sweden from Copenhagen, where he worked with Neils Bohr. It was there that she received the letter.

Meitner and Frisch took long walks in the snow and discussed these exciting results.[3] Eventually, Frisch realized that they

---

[3] Frisch, O. R. How It All Began. *Physics Today* **1967**, *20*, 43.

A representation of the liquid-drop model of fission from
Rhodes' *The Making of the Atomic Bomb*.

fit with Bohr's liquid-drop model of the nucleus. This model predicted that the strong force holding the nucleus together was
gradually cancelled out by the strong repulsion of the protons in
the heavier atoms, thus explaining why there were no stable elements above atomic number 92 (uranium). Furthermore, Frisch
and Meitner immediately realized that, if the nucleus was split,
the positively charged daughter nuclei would be pushed apart by
a strong repulsive force, which they calculated to be 200 MeV
(chemical reactions, on the other hand, release only about 5 eV
per atom).

Meitner and Frisch were excited, but Frisch wanted to run all
of this by Bohr, which he did on returning to Copenhagen. Bohr
instantly accepted the result: "Oh, what idiots we have all been!
Oh, but this is wonderful! This is just as it must be." Bohr, however, could not discuss this result for long because he was leaving
for the United States to spend time at the Institute of Advanced
Studies in Princeton. Frisch immediately set up an experiment to
observe the release of energy in fission. Uranium irradiated with
neutrons released strongly ionizing particles, the fission products, which could be detected in an ionization chamber. The
amount of energy released was close to what had been predicted.

On reaching New York, Bohr was met by a number of
refugee scientists, including Enrico Fermi and Leo Szilard. Soon

At the Department of Terrestrial Magnetism, January 28, 1939.
From left to right: Robert Meyer, Merle Tuve, Enrico Fermi, Richard Roberts,
Leon Rosenfeld, Erik Bohr, Niels Bohr, Gregory Breit, and John Fleming
(Carnegie Institution of Washington archives).

everyone at Princeton and Columbia knew about fission (though
Bohr did not explicitly relay Frisch's result), and excitement was in
the air. Herbert Anderson, a young physicist working at Columbia, set up an experiment equivalent to the one Frisch had done in
Copenhagen. However, before Fermi could hear the result, Bohr
and Fermi left New York for Washington to attend a conference
on theoretical physics at George Washington University that was
sponsored, in part, by the Carnegie Institution of Washington's
Department of Terrestrial Magnetism, chaired by Merle Tuve.
One of Tuve's fellows, Richard Roberts, who was sitting in the
back row, heard Bohr open the conference by relaying the news of

fission from Germany. Fermi discussed its implications. Roberts then returned immediately to the lab to attempt to detect the high-energy fission products of uranium. Roberts reported what happened in a letter to his father:

> We have had a very exciting week in physics. The annual theoretical conference started Thursday with an announcement by Bohr that Hahn in Germany had discovered a radioactive isotope of barium as a product of bombarding uranium with neutrons. Fermi also discussed the reaction and described an obvious experiment to test the theory. The remarkable thing is that this reaction results in 200 million volts of energy liberated and brings back the possibility of atomic power. Hafstad and I left the meeting as soon as Fermi finished to go back to the lab to try the reaction. We had some trouble with a leak in the tube, so it wasn't till Saturday afternoon that Meyers and I finally made the test. We had uranium in our ionization chamber and bombarded it with neutrons. We soon observed tremendous pulses corresponding to very large energy releases. I told Tuve after supper, and he immediately called Bohr and Fermi. They came out Saturday night, we ran the test again for them, and they were immediately convinced. What we did, of course, is of no particular credit to us, but it is nice to be the first to observe the actual splitting of a uranium atom.[4]

Roberts did not know then that his was the third such confirmation, all three of them coming less than a month after Hahn and Strassmann had submitted their paper.

No one at Berkeley yet knew this result, but the news was published in the *Washington Evening Star* and picked up on the AP wire by the *San Francisco Chronicle*.

---

[4] Britten, Roy J. Richard Brooke Roberts. *National Academy of Sciences Biographical Memoirs* **1993**, *62*, 326.

In late January 1939, I made an intense, prolonged irradiation of uranium, isolated the three-day activity in a tiny amount of precipitate, and placed it on my x-ray spectrometer. On January 27th, before the exposure was complete, Luis Alvarez burst into the Radiation Lab with the news that the *Chronicle* contained a story about the discovery of uranium fission. At that moment, I was operating the cyclotron. The news left me stunned. For a whole day, I was intellectually paralyzed. The next morning, I hastened to my laboratory and proceeded to identify the x-ray spectrogram by the use of critical absorption measurements. I then identified the 2.4-hour activity as an iodine isotope. On about February 1st, a short letter was sent to *The Physical Review*. It was received February 3rd and published in the February 15th issue.

Cleavage of the Uranium Nucleus

We have been studying what seemed to be L x-rays from the seventy-two-hour "transuranic" element. These have now been shown by critical absorption measurements to be iodine K x-rays. The seventy-two-hour period is definitely due to tellurium as shown by chemical test, and its daughter substance of two-and-a-half-hour half-life is separated quantitatively as iodine. This seems to be an unambiguous and independent proof of Hahn's hypothesis of the cleavage of the uranium nucleus.

PHILIP ABELSON

University of California,
Berkeley, California,
February 3, 1939.

During the next two months, I moved rapidly to identify antimony, tellurium, and iodine products of uranium fission.

THE
PHYSICAL REVIEW

A Journal of Experimental and Theoretical Physics Established by E. L. Nichols in 1893

VOL. 56, No. 1   JULY 1, 1939   SECOND SERIES

An Investigation of the Products of the Disintegration of Uranium by Neutrons

PHILIP ABELSON
Radiation Laboratory, University of California, Berkeley California
(Received May 11, 1939)

Products of uranium fission which are chemically antimony, tellurium and iodine have been examined. The following activities have been found:

Antimony	Tellurium	Iodine	Atomic Weight
80 hr.	10 hr.		127
4.2 hr.	70 min.		129
	30 min.	8 days	131
	30 hr.		
5 min.	77 hr.	2.4 hr.	132, 134 or 136
<10 min.	43 min.	54 min.	
<10 min.	60 min.	22 hr.	

Three activities—the 10-hour tellurium, the 70-minute tellurium, and the 8-day iodine—have been identified with known bodies through comparison of half-lives and beta-ray spectra. Genetical relationships of the activities have been established by a technique of periodic separations and by the observation of growth in activity curves.

The results were incorporated into an article that *The Physical Review* published on July 1, 1939, as the lead article in volume 56. During April of 1939, I defended my thesis, which was based on the fission work, and I was formally awarded the Ph.D. degree at commencement on May 8th of that year.

This brilliant series of experiments required skill and experience in chemistry, Phil's real strength, and they could not have

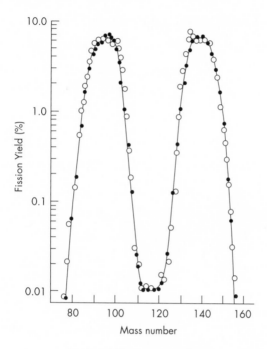

Fission yield vs. mass number.

been done by anyone else in Lawrence's lab at the time. In fact, fission gives rise to a very large number of smaller nuclei, as shown in the graph of fission yield vs. mass number.

Upon receiving my Ph.D., the moment had come for me to think about the future. As a research assistant, I had been receiving $750 a year, but I felt that, if I were to stay at Berkeley, I should be given a raise. Positions elsewhere were scarce at that time, but I thought that, given my accomplishments, I might well be able to get one. One day in June, I called on Ernest Lawrence in his office. I asked him what he intended to do for me. He told me that he would pay me at the rate of $800 a year. I said quietly that I had hoped for more. Lawrence reacted coldly. He told me I was "big-headed" and that he was cutting me off the payroll. That was the end of the encounter. Years later, as I searched through my memory of the incident and its immediate sequelae, I was a bit surprised that I found little or no residue of resentment. At any rate, I remained until September at the Radiation Lab and completed a paper on x rays emitted during radioactive decay.

Following the publication of his paper in *The Physical Review*, Phil received several job offers, including one from Harvard and one from Washington University, but he accepted an offer from Merle Tuve to join the Laboratory of Terrestrial Magnetism at the Carnegie Institution of Washington at a salary of $2900 per year! His first job there was to supervise the construction of a 60-inch cyclotron. He arrived in September of 1939, and he was associated with that institution for the rest of his life.

5

The First Artificial Element

In Washington Phil began work on the new cyclotron, but he was following the rapid developments as physicists everywhere began to consider the implications of nuclear fission. It was immediately considered likely that neutrons would be released in nuclear fission and that if two neutrons were released in each fission event then a chain reaction could occur. Although it took time to confirm this possibility, several groups (including Enrico Fermi's and, independently, Leo Szilard and Walter Zinn) confirmed that excess neutrons (approximately two) were liberated in the fission reaction. Thus, an atomic bomb became a possibility.

Natural uranium is a mixture of three isotopes: ^{238}U (99.276%), ^{235}U (0.718%), and ^{234}U (0.0056%). Bohr proposed, on theoretical grounds, that only ^{235}U underwent fission and, with the purification of minute amounts of ^{235}U by mass spectrometry, this too was later confirmed. The next step was to demonstrate that a chain reaction could in fact occur. Working at Columbia University, Enrico Fermi and Leo Szilard attempted to do just that.

In 1939, with Germany forcefully appropriating Czechoslovakia, it was clear (to the refugee scientists, at least) that war was at hand and that German scientists would be well equipped and perhaps motivated to put the power of nuclear fission to destructive use. A formidable trio of Hungarians—Leo Szilard, Edward Teller, and Eugene Wigner—decided that the American government must be warned of this possibility. In order to do this most effectively, they eventually recruited Albert Einstein to sign a letter they had written to President Roosevelt describing the implications of nuclear fission. This letter was carried to the president by Alexander Sachs, an economist who knew Roosevelt.

Written in August, 1939, the letter finally reached Roosevelt's office in October. By this time, Germany had invaded Poland, and Britain and France had entered the war. This was a busy period for Roosevelt and it had taken a long time for Sachs to get an appointment with him. Roosevelt immediately understood the situation and a committee was formed under the chairmanship of Lyman Briggs, the director of the Bureau of Standards, with representatives from the Army and Navy.

The first meeting of the committee was held on October 21, 1939, with scientific representatives including Szilard, Teller, and Wigner. Merle Tuve was invited, but he sent Richard Roberts in his place. This meeting was important because it was the first time Americans had considered building an atomic bomb and it was to set the tone for the government's response to the idea during the next two years. The military was skeptical and Roberts was not yet convinced that a chain reaction would take place. Teller, however, asked for financial support for the work that Szilard and Fermi had started at Columbia. Teller was asked how much support would be needed. In this, the first grant request for government support of big science, the request was for $6000 to buy some pure graphite, which was needed to moderate neutron emission in the nuclear reactor.

The discovery that the main products of the neutron irradiation of uranium were fission products discredited Fermi's claim of the discovery of ekarhenium, element 93, but the discovery of fission did not eliminate the possibility that transuranic elements might exist. Remarkably, Phil was to discover the first of these elements.

In September 1939, coming on the train from Tacoma to take up my new position in Washington, DC, the Germans invaded Poland. Everybody in the lab was nervous but didn't know what to do. While I did do some work on the cyclotron, ordering parts and so on, I also began thinking about uranium (particularly a product that McMillan had been studying). When he irradiated uranium with neutrons he observed not only fission products, such as rubidium and iodine, but also a 23-minute beta-*emitting* isotope of uranium (^{239}U). This radioactivity had been observed well ahead of the discovery of fission. It was inferred that decay of the isotope gave rise to a transuranic element number 93.

In the spring of 1939, following the announcement of fission, Ed McMillan began a series of elegant experiments at Berkeley in which he captured the products of fission in a stack of thin foils. Eventually cigarette papers were found to work in this experiment. Depending on its energy, a particular fission product would penetrate through the stack, lodging in a characteristic layer. This experiment confirmed that there were a number of different fission products, but the interesting thing was that at least two radioactive products remained with the uranium. These products could not even penetrate a stack of cigarette papers. One product, with a half-life of 23 minutes, was known to be ^{239}U; it was the result of neutron capture by ^{238}U. The other product, with a half-life of 2.3 days, could be the product of beta decay of the first product, and would therefore be element 93. Emilio Segrè (originally an associate of Fermi's in Rome but then in Berkeley) set about to characterize the 2.3-day product.

> He expected its properties to be similar to rhenium. Segre was very familiar with the chemistry of this element, since he and his co-workers had discovered another of its homologs, technetium. He showed that the 2.3-day material had none of the properties of rhenium, and indeed acted like a rare earth. Since rare earths are prominent among the fission products, this discovery seemed at the time to end the story.[1]

Segrè published this negative result in June 1939, and there the matter might have stood.

In January 1940, I reread the Segrè letter and was immediately and strongly of the opinion that the 2.3-day activity was that of a transuranic element. I began studying what to do about it. I found out that in the middle of the periodic table you have lanthanum that, when radioactive, decays to cerium. Lanthanum is the first rare earth element and cerium is the next and they are normally valence three. But with a powerful oxidizing agent, cerium can be oxidized to valence four. So, I began thinking this may well be the key to identifying the product. Fermi had called it ekarhenium, implying that it would have properties like rhenium. Well, but

---

[1] E. M. McMillan, Nobel Lecture, December 12, 1951.

what if instead of it behaving like Fermi had supposed, suppose you had a new rare earth series. Well, then the way of snipping this thing out would be to subject the uranium product of powerful neutron irradiation to a powerful oxidant and see what happens.[2]

I approached Merle Tuve with these thoughts, and he was interested. He was concerned, however, that if I were to conduct chemical experiments with uranium on the DTM premises, the background count would be raised, which would cause trouble for others in the lab trying to detect low levels of radioactivity. He arranged for lab space at American University with Sterling Hendricks. Tuve also obtained platinum dishes from the Geophysical Laboratory that enabled me to conduct fluoride precipitations in acid solution.

Lawrence Hafstad conducted some neutron irradiations for me using the Van de Graaf generator, which was then operating at only about 2 MeV and a few microamperes. The compound irradiated was uranyl nitrate $[UO_2(NO_3)_2]$. The two irradiations and subsequent chemistry produced disappointing results. The amount of radioactivity was very small in comparison with what I had known in Berkeley, and the chemical separations gave inconsistent results. I concluded that, if I were to make further progress, I needed to have the beam intensities available at Berkeley.

———————

[2] Much of this paragraph is from the oral history taken by Amy Crumpton.

When Phil left Berkeley in 1939, Neva remained there because she was still attending medical school in San Francisco. Thus, when he returned to see her in the spring of 1940, he took that opportunity to continue his search for transuranic elements.

When I arrived there about May 10th, I found that McMillan was still interested in the 2.3-day activity, and he quickly agreed to irradiate another thin film of ammonium uranate [$(NH_4)_2U_2O_7$] and to arrange for chemicals, platinum ware, and laboratory space for me to use. Within a few hours after my arrival in Berkeley, I conducted the crucial experiment. In the presence of bromate (BrO_3^-), a strong oxidizing agent, the activity did not precipitate with cerium in acid. When the solution was made to be reducing and more cerium was added, the precipitate contained the 2.3-day activity.

On the basis of this result, it was possible to conduct confirmatory experiments in which large amounts of uranium were irradiated and the 2.3-day activity was isolated free of fission products. This made it possible to explore the other chemical properties of the substance. It became clear that element 93 represented one of a new series of rare earths, and this was confirmed and extended by the later creation of higher transuranic elements. For example, element 93 behaved like thorium (element 90) in the reduced state and like uranyl uranium (oxidation state +6) in the oxidized state.

Edwin McMillan recreating the isolation of
neptunium for a news photo in 1940.

It was possible to prove a genetic relationship between the
23-minute and the 2.3-day activities. In total, I spent five days in
Berkeley, part of which was devoted to writing up the letter that
appeared in an issue of *The Physical Review* in June 1940.

To me an interesting and amazing aspect of this story is that the insight to control the oxidation state of the product derived from Phil's conjecture that the periodic table as drawn in 1939 was wrong. In that periodic table element 93 is just below rhenium (element 75) and would be predicted to have similar chemical properties to rhenium.

In the present day periodic table, the actinides form a new rare-earth-like series starting with actinium (element 89) and are predicted to have physical and chemical properties similar to the lanthanides (elements 57 through 70). Phil must have been the first person to have this insight, though the actinide series itself was proposed later by Glenn Seaborg.

The following nuclear equations summarize what was known at this point:

$$^{238}_{92}U + n \rightarrow {}^{239}_{92}U$$

$$\overset{30 \text{ min}}{^{239}_{92}U \rightarrow {}^{239}_{93}Np + e^-}$$

$$\overset{2.3 \text{ days}}{^{239}_{93}Np \rightarrow {}^{239}_{94}X + e^-}$$

Left unanswered by this work was the nature of the ^{239}Np decay product ($^{239}_{94}X$). Without access to the cyclotron, Phil was unable to pursue this question. McMillan, moreover, had left Berkeley to join the radar-development project at MIT, so the characterization of the decay product was left to the chemist Glenn Seaborg. In a series of exhaustive radiochemical experiments, Seaborg and his collaborators learned to purify neptunium. Two isotopes of the decay product were eventually isolated, $^{238}_{94}X$ and $^{239}_{94}X$.

By March 1941, Seaborg and his collaborators had shown that $^{239}_{94}X$ underwent fission when irradiated with slow neutrons. As a result, element 94, later named plutonium, could also be used to

Glenn Seaborg, Philip Abelson, and Edwin McMillan (left to right) at the 50th anniversary of the cyclotron at the Lawrence Berkeley Lab (ca. 1980).

create a nuclear chain reaction. In fact, ^{239}Pu has a higher cross section for neutron capture than ^{235}U and is thus more fissionable. With this result, the outlines of the atomic bomb project were established. On the one hand ^{235}U could be purified from ^{238}U, although it was difficult because they both have the same chemical properties. On the other hand, ^{239}Pu could be purified from the products of the neutron irradiation of uranium. This was conceptually simpler, because the unique chemical properties of plutonium could be exploited. It was also difficult, though, because it turned out that Pu was present in the complex mixture of radiation products at a level of 250 parts per million. Remarkably, Phil's contributions had been crucial to both approaches.

6

A Manhattan Project
of His Own

During Phil's return trip from Berkeley to Washington in mid-May 1940, Germany invaded France. Saturation bombing of English cities had begun with huge loss of life. War seemed inevitable. Phil had a lot of time on the transcontinental train to consider what he should do. The previous year, just before he had left for Washington, Phil had been in Oppenheimer's office, perhaps discussing his thesis. Oppenheimer drew a rough sketch of a ^{235}U gun assembly on the blackboard and told Phil that a weapon of that design was theoretically feasible but practical only if an industrial-scale method of separating the ^{235}U isotope could be developed.[1] Phil had not acted on that suggestion in 1939 but now with the war more imminent he was led to consider this route.

---

[1] This story comes from Peter Vogel who has studied Phil's career in conjunction with his thesis that a huge explosion at Port Chicago on San Francisco Bay in 1944 was a nuclear explosion. Phil told the story to Vogel in a telephone interview. Although Vogel's thesis is not believable, it is plausible that Phil talked with Oppenheimer about his nuclear fission results. For more on Vogel's views, consult www.portchicago.org.

When he arrived back in Washington, the staff at the Department of Terrestrial Magnetism had also begun to consider how they should respond to the situation in Europe. Tuve and Roberts began experiments that led to the discovery of the proximity fuze[2] and ultimately to its successful manufacture and deployment in weapons. Phil assessed his talents and decided to begin the ^{235}U enrichment project.

I soon decided that I should examine the feasibility of large-scale separation of uranium isotopes. That was a very ambitious goal at the time, though, because methods of separating heavy isotopes were primitive and the yields were trivial. After a survey of the literature, I chose liquid thermal diffusion as the method to explore.

At this point at least three methods had been considered for the separation of uranium isotopes. Several groups in England and the United States, for example, were working on gaseous diffusion. Lawrence, on the other hand, had proposed building huge mass spectrometers—essentially separating the isotopes atom by atom. Finally, there was the possibility of using centrifugation. Liquid thermal diffusion, the approach Phil decided to explore, was not initially considered by the Manhattan project. (It was learned after the war, however, that a Japanese group had embarked on this same approach.) Although Phil had decided on

---

[2] To learn more about proximity fuzes, consult www.history.navy.mil/faqs/faq96–1.htm. This is a Navy historical website that describes the development of the proximity fuze.

his approach, it was uncertain how much material would have to be purified. That depended on the critical mass required to support a chain reaction, and this had been calculated variously as being between 10 kg and 1000 kg of ^{235}U. To start this project required an enormous leap of faith.

The original work on liquid thermal diffusion had been conducted by H. Korsching and Karl Wirtz in Germany.[3] They discovered that partial separations could be accomplished when aqueous zinc solutions were subjected to a thermal gradient in a column. The main components of liquid thermal diffusion columns were three concentric pipes. The inner pipe was supplied with a heat source such as steam. A space between the inner and a second, middle pipe contained the working substance. Around the second pipe was a third one, which served as an outer jacket for cooling fluids.

In the thermal gradient the lighter isotope diffuses marginally toward the hot and the heavier isotope towards the cold. The heating and the cooling of the sample causes a convection gradient up the hot pipe wall and down the cold so that the lower atomic weight isotope migrates to the top of the column and the heavier isotope to the bottom. After the column reaches equilibrium, the partially purified heavy isotope can be decanted from the bottom of the column.

----

[3] Korsching, H.; Wirtz, K. *Naturwissenschaften* **1939**, *27*, 110 and *Naturwissenschaften* **1939**, *27*, 367.

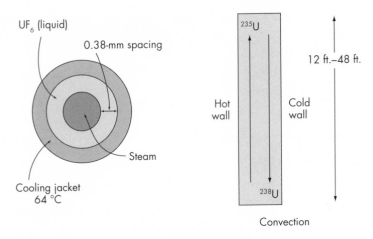

Liquid thermal diffusion.

Iapplied the German technique to soluble potassium salts and obtained an isotope separation. But, when an aqueous solution of a uranium salt was used, an insoluble mess appeared at the bottom of the column. Laboratory colleagues noticed this result and Merle Tuve soon learned of it, too. He again believed that I was likely to contaminate the Carnegie facilities with a high background level of radioactivity, so he immediately began to look for a place for me to do my uranium research elsewhere.

Lyman J. Briggs, the director of the National Bureau of Standards (NBS), had already been named chairman of the Uranium Committee by President Roosevelt. The Uranium Committee was the top federal group making decisions about support of nuclear uranium research. Those serving with him on the committee included Merle Tuve; Ross Gunn, Chief Technical Advisor, Naval Research Laboratory; George Pegram, Columbia University; and Jesse Beams, an expert on ultracentrifugation at the University of Virginia.

Tuve met with Dr. Briggs to negotiate the change of locale for my uranium research. Briggs quickly made space available for me at the NBS.

When I arrived at the National Bureau of Standards I was provided with a large room to house my experiments on liquid thermal diffusion. I was also given space to conduct the synthesis of uranium compounds that would be suitable as working fluids for my experimental equipment. I soon decided to synthesize uranium hexafluoride (UF_6), a volatile compound that was not commercially available. Small amounts of it had been prepared previously by passing fluorine over powders of uranium metal.

Uranium tetrafluoride (UF_4) could be prepared from cheap and abundant raw materials, and I successfully prepared it. Relying on my mechanical experience, I constructed a fluorine generator using the shop at Tuve's lab. Back at the NBS, I was soon producing UF_6 by exposing dry UF_4 to fluorine at a temperature of 250 °C. I synthesized about 10 kilograms of UF_6 there. Later I received a patent on the process for which, allegedly, the government of the United States graciously paid me one dollar. That dollar I never clutched.

Phil's facility for producing UF_6 was the first in the country and the only source of UF_6 through all of 1941, so during that period they supplied the entire uranium research effort with UF_6.

After I had produced substantial amounts of UF_6, I conducted experiments at the NBS to determine its stability at high temperatures. I also examined the reactivity of UF_6 with various metals at high temperatures.

Uranium hexafluoride melts at 64 °C. Its vapor pressure at that temperature is more than one atmosphere. The compound is highly reactive. It is hydrolyzed by water and it reacts rapidly with organic matter. Nickel withstood exposure to UF_6 at temperatures as high as 500 °C. Copper was suitable at 64 °C. I found that the ability of substances to resist attack by UF_6 was enhanced by a conditioning process that involved pretreatment with fluorine gas.

With these chemical properties of uranium hexafluoride known, it was possible for me, with some confidence, to build and operate a liquid thermal diffusion column. Runs on a 12-foot-long column were made in April 1941. The results showed a small separation.

––––––––––

At this point the measurements of isotope separation were done by Alfred Nier at the University of Minnesota using a special mass spectrometer that he had designed. Later the Navy built their own mass spectrometer based on the Nier design.

As a member of the Uranium Committee, Ross Gunn was informed of the separation of uranium isotopes that had been achieved. He knew that higher steam temperatures were available at the Naval Research Laboratory, so the isotope work was moved there in June of 1941.

———————

Gunn's motivation for bringing Phil to the Naval Research Laboratory (NRL) derived from his own early conviction, even before the discovery of fission, that atomic energy could be used to power a submarine. With a conventional power plant, the submarine must frequently surface to obtain the oxygen needed to burn fuel, a maneuver that compromises the safety of the submarine. Gunn was immediately aware of the significance of the announcement of nuclear fission in January of 1939 and approached the director of the NRL, Rear Admiral Harold Bowen, with the proposal to initiate work on nuclear fission with the specific goal of submarine propulsion. Fifteen hundred dollars was allotted for this purpose.[4]

Ross Gunn, chief technical advisor of the Naval Research Laboratory and member of the Uranium Committee, as he appeared circa 1950.

———————

[4] Bowen, Harold G. *Ships, Machinery and Mossbacks*; Princeton University Press: Princeton, NJ, 1954; p. 182.

During my nine-month stay at the NBS, Lyman J. Briggs often called on me for advice on nuclear matters. I was immediately available and I was acquainted with some of the scientists that he had not yet met. On one occasion, for instance, I drafted a letter for him to Glenn Seaborg in which Seaborg (then at the University of California, Berkeley) was granted a substantial sum to conduct studies involving plutonium. On several other occasions I visited industrial laboratories to obtain information useful to Dr. Briggs.

This contact with Briggs and others associated with the Uranium Committee was to be Phil's only source of information about what was going on in the rest of the United States' effort to build an atomic bomb.

At the NRL, 100-psi steam was available that could provide heat for a longer diffusion column. The combination of these two features led to better isotope separations. Experiments were conducted to discover the optimum spacing between the hot and cold walls of a 36-foot column. Ultimately a high-pressure boiler was obtained that produced steam at 1,000 psi and a temperature of 286 °C. In June 1942 a column with a spacing of 0.038 centimeters gave a separation factor of 1.11[5] with a halftime of 12 hours.

---

[5] The separation factor is the ratio of the fraction of ^{235}U to ^{238}U after the separation compared to the ratio of the fraction before the separation. Thus, the enrichment process with a separation factor of 1.11 increased the fraction of ^{235}U in the sample from 0.0072 to 0.0080.

Further experiments yielded larger separation factors at 0.025 centimeters. While this optimum value was established, encouraging experience was gained in operating liquid thermal diffusion columns. It turned out that the equipment was easy to operate. By cutting columns apart we determined that little corrosion had occurred. These favorable circumstances led to a decision to increase the scope of the work at the NRL by building a 14-column pilot plant. Work on this plant was authorized in July 1942.

In 1940, after Germany invaded Western Europe, the administration of military research changed and was under the direction of a new agency, the Office of Scientific Research and Development (OSRD). This civilian agency, charged with engineering development of military research, was conceived and directed by Vannevar Bush, then the president of the Carnegie Institution of Washington. The civilian direction of the atomic fission project was in the hands of the S-1 Committee of the OSRD chaired by James Conant, then president of Harvard University. At first this committee was the Uranium Committee, but this group was gradually phased out and with it any Navy representation in the oversight of the nuclear fission project.

According to Admiral Bowen, "This new group [Conant et al.] moved in on the original committee of active workers and evidently took charge because by April, 1942, they had issued orders to 'hold reports' . . . without distribution to members of the Section S-1." The effect of this order was to deprive the Naval Research Laboratory of all information regarding developments in atomic energy (for what reasons, I don't know). The fault, though, may have been in the Navy's high command because at one stage, after the news got around Washington about the large disbursements of the Manhattan Engineering District, there were many who thought that the whole thing would be a flop, were afraid of the day of reckoning, and didn't want to be involved in it. Whatever the reason, the Naval Research Laboratory, which employed Drs. Gunn and Abelson, the first two people in government service to work on atomic energy, was prevented from participating in this great and successful effort, except for the one instance cited (i.e., the eventual incorporation of the liquid thermal diffusion method).[6,7]

Work on atomic fission at this time was largely confined to attempts at demonstrating the chain reaction. After the Japanese attacked Pearl Harbor on December 7, 1941, and the United States entered the war, the execution of the nuclear fission project became the responsibility of the U.S. Army and support for the project was dramatically increased. The S-1 Committee continued to give civilian advice, but the project was made secret and was moved to the University of Chicago under the overall direction of Arthur Compton. By December 1942, the graphite-moderated nuclear reactor at the University of Chicago had been constructed in the squash court under Stagg Field and on the cold day of December 2nd, Fermi calmly brought it to criticality. It ran for four minutes and was shut down by the insertion of cadmium modulator rods.

---

[6] Bowen, Harold G. *Ships, Machinery and Mossbacks*; Princeton University Press: Princeton, NJ, 1954; p. 187.

[7] "Van (Bush) excluded the Navy as an act of sheer bias. . . . The Navy had shown an interest in fission since 1939, primarily because it might offer a new power source for submarines, and the Navy hired the first two people paid by the government to investigate fission. Yet Van blocked its participation. . . . Van had his reasons. The Navy saw NRDC as a threat, and its top officers ignored him. . . . But Army leaders consulted him frequently." Source: Zachary, G. P. Vannevar Bush backs the bomb. *Bulletin of the Atomic Scientists* **1992**, *48*, 24.

The S-1 Committee at Bohemian Grove, California (left to right):
Harold Urey, Ernest Lawrence, James Conant, Lyman Briggs, E. V. Murphree,
and Arthur Compton.

In September 1942, General Leslie Groves of the Army
Corps of Engineers was appointed to direct the Manhattan Project and at that point it took off. Groves immediately bought all of
the uranium ore in the United States and attempted to monopo-
lize the world supply. During the next year Groves organized the
Manhattan Project as an enormous three-part effort. The atomic
bomb was to be designed and assembled at Los Alamos, New
Mexico, under the direction of Robert Oppenheimer. Uranium
isotopes were to be separated at massive plants at Oak Ridge,
Tennessee, employing both gaseous barrier diffusion and
Lawrence's enormous mass spectrometers. Large reactors were
constructed at Hanford, Washington near the Columbia River

and remote-control plants were constructed to separate plutonium from the highly radioactive fission products. Under a security program called "compartmentalization," the scientists in
each of these plants did not know, in general, what was going on
elsewhere.

M y efforts at the NRL were conducted in collaboration with
and were facilitated by Ross Gunn. As Chief Technical
Advisor to the naval officer commanding the laboratory, Gunn
had clout.

———————

After the war, Gunn reported on this phase of the effort to a
Senate committee:

> Upon his [Phil's] transfer [from the Bureau of Standards], John I.
> Hoover and four other assistants were assigned to his work. With
> the aid of top priorities in the shop, a number of experimental
> columns were fabricated and operated under many different con-
> ditions with UF_6 as the active material. By November 15, 1942,
> more than 10 different columns had been evaluated, and the
> results showed that the method was entirely successful.[8]

I t was the policy of the Naval Research Laboratory to commu-
nicate results to the Uranium Committee and later to the Manhattan District as soon as information was available. Accordingly,

———————

[8] U.S. Senate Committee on Atomic Energy. *Atomic Energy: Hearings Pursuant to S. Res. 179*,
79th Congress (1st session), 13, 14, 19, and 20 December 1945.

in August 1942, Gunn informed Lyman J. Briggs of the new developments regarding the separation process. This led to a visit in December by General Leslie R. Groves, head of the Manhattan District, together with Admiral W. R. Purnell. Later, in January 1943, the installation was inspected by a special committee assembled by the Manhattan District. The committee was impressed by the simplicity of the equipment and commented favorably. No action was taken.

The S-1 advisory committee that visited the NRL in January 1943 consisted of Lyman Briggs (chairman), E. V. Murphree of Standard Oil Development Co., and Harold Urey of Columbia University. Karl Cohen and W. I. Thompson accompanied them as advisors. The committee was impressed:

> It is felt that the Naval Research Laboratory has developed a simple and positive means of separating the uranium isotope and this method, at least qualitatively, has been well demonstrated. There would appear to be no major mechanical problems to be solved. The thermal diffusion process as developed has the very great advantage of mechanical simplicity.

The committee, however, considering the time and cost needed to use this method alone to accumulate sufficient weapons-grade uranium, estimated that it would take 600 days, following an 18-month period to build the plant at a cost of $75,000,000 (about the cost estimated for the alternate approaches). The combined time—almost three and a half years—seemed too long. The committee, though, did consider using diffusion as a first-stage purification: "The time to come to equilibrium may prove to be too long

for use of this method for the whole process, but still it may be possible to use the process for the lower part of the plant."

> The method seems to be remarkably free from many of the trou-
> bles that we experience in the other methods.

The committee took the liquid thermal diffusion method
seriously, because they issued a separate memo pointing out that
it was the Germans who had invented liquid thermal diffusion, so
they would have had a running start in applying this procedure to
the uranium separation process. If the Germans had started in
1940, the committee reckoned they could possibly have obtained
weapons-grade material by 1943. As a result, the committee gave
the following set of instructions for reconnaissance units:

> The plant or plants would be placed in a coal mining region
> where some five or ten thousand tons of coal a day would be
> available. Some 30,000 kilowatts of electrical power would be
> required for the total of all the units. These plants must be placed
> either on a river to furnish the necessary cooling water or else
> they will have water cooling towers. The plants will undoubtedly
> be heavily camouflaged and might conceivably be built into the
> side of a hill.

The committee went on to describe the size of the plant and
to suggest that I. G. Farbenindustrie might be the operator. They
concluded, "This committee would be glad to study photographs
of any plants which are being built in Germany."[9]

The S-1 Committee report was forwarded to General
Groves, but no action was taken regarding the work being done
at the NRL except to request a further visit by virtually the same
committee.

---

[9] National Archives: Records of the Office of Scientific Research and Development, Record
Group 227, Bush–Conant file, microfilm reel 9, frames 622–634 (both letters).

After this visit Conant made concrete recommendations in a letter sent September 15, 1943 to Rear Admiral W. R. Purnell (a member of the Military Policy Committee of the OSRD):

> . . . [I]t would be most unfortunate for the entire effort if any further expansion of the work of the Naval Research Laboratory in this field were to result in the drawing away of personnel now being employed on other aspects of this program. In particular, we had in mind such men as Drs. Beams, Nye, Armistead, Snoddy and Ham of the University of Virginia. (There had been a collaboration between the NRL and this group from the very start of its project in 1939.) . . . [T]he most useful role of the NRL would be a careful study, on a small scale, of the problems referred to in this report.
>
> [In addition,] we understand that there is still available at the Naval Research Laboratory approximately 80 pounds of hex [UF6]. . . . If this material . . can be made available to those now engaged on the project under the general direction of the Military Policy Committee for experimental purposes, the favor will be deeply appreciated, and an equivalent amount of base material will be supplied in exchange.[10]

Base material (uranium oxide), however, was withheld from the Navy for some time. This was clearly an attempt to squelch the NRL effort.

Phil was circumspect about the failure of Groves and the Manhattan District to appreciate the successful efforts in isotope separation at the NRL. In his later testimony, however, Gunn (not circumspect) revealed an active policy of the Manhattan Project to hinder progress at the NRL:

> One of the serious difficulties at that time was the preparation of adequate supplies of UF6. . . . Dr. Abelson worked out a practicable method for its production on a large scale and this permitted

---

[10]National Archives: Records of the Office of Scientific Research and Development, Record Group 227, Bush–Conant file, microfilm reel 10, frames 152–153.

the laboratory to satisfy its own demands. The Manhattan District was anxious to use the method in their system and we were asked to turn this valuable information over to the Harshaw Chemical Co. This was done on December 1, 1941. Later the Manhattan District rewarded our strenuous efforts to advance the uranium power program by ordering the War Production Board in November 1943 to withhold from the NRL the supplies of UF6 to operate our . . . plant. It took months of effort, in the midst of war, to get this sordid and incredible political action reversed. . . .

The Manhattan District missed no opportunity to scuttle the NRL program and no useful assistance was ever obtained from them. On the other hand, NRL kept the District informed in every way. As an example General Groves visited our pilot plant on December 10, 1942, and was given access to all our results. The next month an advisory group from the District visited the laboratory and made a favorable report on our process, but this information and recommendation was placed in cold storage and the important relation of our work to the national uranium effort was not examined for much more than a year. It is my view that this action prolonged the war by many months. The Navy must share some of the blame for this failure because the top Navy representation in the national program was weak and ineffective.[11]

During the next six months improvements were made in column construction. The small pilot plant produced some 236 pounds of uranium hexafluoride enriched in ^{235}U. The product was sent to Chicago. The quantity and the extent of isotope

---

[11]Testimony to U.S. Senate Committee on Atomic Energy. See footnote 7. See also Ahern, Joseph-James. "We had the hose turned on us!": Ross Gunn and The Naval Research Laboratory's Early Research into Nuclear Propulsion, 1939–1946. *International Journal of Naval History* **2003**, *2(1)*.

separation were greater than had been obtained from the gaseous diffusion method up to that time.

What was Phil's personal life like during the war? During that period he had several different rooms in Washington and likely spent some weekends with Aunt Neva in Baltimore where she was a medical student at Johns Hopkins. But likely he spent most nights at the lab because much later when he was director of the Geophyscial Laboratory that is exactly what he did, sleeping on a cot in a room near his office. Amy Crumpton of the AAAS asked him about communication with Aunt Neva about his project during the war years:

> Amy Crumpton: "Did you ever speak about your work to your wife?"
>
> Phil: "Oh, no, no, no, no. No, it was no use. How was that going to benefit the war effort?"
>
> Crumpton: "Did you feel isolated?"
>
> Phil: "No, I didn't feel isolated."
>
> Crumpton: "You were getting some interesting results."
>
> Phil: "I knew what I wanted to do, what I could do, and I knew what experiments I ought to be doing."

The Naval Research Laboratory decided to expand its isotope studies with the objective of providing an alternative method in the event that the magnetic or gaseous diffusion methods failed. We regarded our work as insurance against this possibility. A survey of naval establishments indicated that the Naval

Boiler and Turbine Laboratory at the Philadelphia Naval Base possessed a number of unique facilities. Building space was available, cooling water could easily be obtained, and the engineers at that laboratory had considerable experience in high-pressure steam and in large-scale heavy construction. Authorization to build a 300-unit pilot plant at Philadelphia was obtained on November 17, 1943 under a project order signed by Rear Admiral Earle Mills, USN, Assistant Chief of the Bureau of Ships. Construction of the installation began about January 1, 1944.

———————————

By this time, the huge separation plants at Oak Ridge were coming on line and initial runs of both were a disaster. In the electromagnetic plant uranium stuck to the walls, vacuums failed, and the output was miniscule. In the diffusion plants, a decision had been made to replace the barrier material, a porous nickel plate, with a nickel powder, necessitating a considerable delay. Despite the policy of compartmentalization, Phil knew of the troubles at Oak Ridge, he knew about Los Alamos, and he knew that Robert Oppenheimer was its director. Thinking that he could assist the process of ^{235}U enrichment, he decided to approach Oppenheimer directly rather than through channels.

When I left the NBS in June 1942, Dr. Briggs obtained a new and better nuclear advisor, a theoretical physicist named Gregory Breit. Breit had earlier collaborated with Merle Tuve. He knew of the isotope separation that had been achieved at the NRL. Breit also knew that a high-ranking naval officer who had been associated with Merle Tuve and his proximity fuze work had been reassigned to work with Oppenheimer's group at Los Alamos. One day in early 1944, I received instructions to prepare a brief summary of the isotope work and to appear at 8 P.M. on the balcony of the Warner Theater in Washington, DC. There I would encounter a naval officer who would whisper a code word. I learned later that the officer immediately traveled to Los Alamos.

The officer Phil met in the Warner Theater was Deak Parsons. Parsons, a munitions expert, had been assigned to Los Alamos to help in the construction and testing of the gun used to initiate the chain reaction in the uranium bomb.

He was forty-three, cool, vigorous, trim and nearly bald, spit-and-polish but innovative; 'all his life', one of the men who worked for him at Los Alamos testifies in praise, 'he fought the silly regulations and conservatism of the Navy'. . . . Parsons was married to Martha Cluverius, a Vassar graduate and the daughter of an admiral. With two blonde daughters and a cocker spaniel, the couple arrived at Los Alamos in an open red convertible.[12]

Deak Parsons (left) and Phil being awarded distinguished service citations by the Navy in 1945.

Later, aboard the Enola Gay, Parsons armed the uranium bomb dropped on Hiroshima.

---

[12]Rhodes, Richard. *The Making of the Atomic Bomb*; Touchstone: New York, 1986.

Richard Rhodes, the author of *The Making of the Atomic Bomb*, asked Phil if (in this incident) he had deliberately breached compartmentalization. "I sure as hell did," he replied. In breaching compartmentalization he apparently had the ideal co-conspirator in Parsons.

Oppenheimer recognized the value that partially separated uranium would have when used as a first-step purification in conjunction with the electromagnetic isotope separation plant at Oak Ridge. At that time the electromagnetic plant was the only large-scale isotope separation unit in operation. The potential of liquid thermal diffusion as a method to increase the rate of production of bomb-grade uranium was brought to the attention of General Groves by Oppenheimer in late April 1944.

After the war Groves testified, "Dr. Oppenheimer . . . suddenly told me that we had made a terrible scientific blunder. I think he was right. We had failed to consider thermal diffusion as a portion of the process as a whole. Rather the strategy had been to pursue gaseous diffusion and mass spectrometry, hoping that one of these processes would succeed in purifying ^{235}U completely."[13]

They had not considered using the processes in tandem, a tactic commonplace in the purification of proteins, for example. Oppenheimer's letter to Groves on April 28, 1944 suggested using thermal diffusion as a feeder process for the electromagnetic sepa-

[13]Groves, Leslie R. *Now it Can Be Told: The Story of the Manhattan Project*; Harper & Brothers Publishers: New York, 1962; p. 120.

ration. Groves did not immediately respond, but after a month finally appointed a committee to visit the Philadelphia facility. Why he continued to be reluctant to involve the Navy in the Manhattan Project is unclear. Perhaps it was a matter of service rivalry or an attempt to limit the agencies involved for security reasons.

In any case, Oppenheimer's and ultimately Grove's reconsideration of the value of liquid thermal diffusion led to considerable agitation on the part of James Conant. Consider the following absurd and pompous memo sent by Conant to Vannevar Bush dated May 6, 1944:

> I uncovered a rather strange and to my mind a rather unpleasant bit of past history in S-1 the other day. In a conversation with Smyth[14] & myself, Briggs was led to recount the origin of the Naval Research Lab's method. According to his story, Abelson (of Carnegie) was working at the Bureau of Standards in the earlier days of the Briggs committee (the Uranium committee) and either invented or developed the idea of thermal liquid diffusion and obtained results indicating that there was a chance that it would work. Gunn, a member of the Briggs committee but apparently no one else became a party to this knowingly and prevailed upon Briggs to let Abelson go to the NRL where they had a lot of steam necessary for the purpose. Gunn and Abelson continued working on the thermal diffusion process at NRL and kept Briggs informed of progress. Briggs felt himself under pledge not to tell anyone else. This continued till Briggs was smoked out by some questions of Urey in the summer of 1943 (my interpretation!) Briggs said that finally he felt he must get a release from the NRL and reveal to the S-1 Executive Committee NRL progress.
>
> I rather led Briggs on in an innocent way to tell this story. From my point of view it is very damaging to Briggs. Whether he

---

[14]Princeton physicist Henry DeWolf Smyth, author of *Atomic Energy for Military Purposes: The Official Report on the Development of the Atomic Bomb Under the Auspices of the United States Government, 1940–1945*; Princeton University Press: Princeton, NJ, 1945.

realized it or not I don't know but I wrote the enclosed letter [20 April, 1944] and have received no reply after two weeks.[15]

I'm not particularly anxious to accuse Briggs of double-dealing nor Gunn either. But I could get very mad in retrospect about his behavior. It is necessary to make a record now to show why the S-1 committee never pushed the Thermal Diffusion method, namely because they were never informed of it?

In particular shall I forget the letter I wrote to Briggs though to me his failure to reply is pretty much an admission of guilt?[16]

Following this, a reviewing committee visited the Philadelphia installation about June 15, 1944. Their report to General Groves was favorable. The decision was made to build a 2142-column liquid thermal diffusion plant at Oak Ridge, employing steam from a powerhouse built for the gaseous diffusion process. Work on the powerhouse had been completed ahead of the gaseous diffusion plant so that steam was available. On June 26, 1944 General Groves, accompanied by Richard Tolman, W. l. Thompson of the Ferguson Corporation, and Lt. Col. M. C. Fox, arrived at the Naval Research Laboratory to obtain any and all such information that was available concerning work on the thermal diffusion process. Blueprints of the Philadelphia installation were turned over to them. General Groves issued instructions

---

[15] The letter from Conant to Briggs dated April 20, 1944 asked Briggs for details on the origin of the research on liquid thermal diffusion.

[16] National Archives: Records of the Office of Scientific Research and Development, Record Group 227, Bush–Conant file, microfilm reel 4, frames 822–823.

The S-50 plant for liquid thermal diffusion in Oak Ridge, Tennessee.

that the Oak Ridge installation was to be built as a "Chinese copy" of the Philadelphia plant.

The speed of construction of the Oak Ridge installation was phenomenal. Ground was broken for what was called the S-50 plant on July 6, 1944, and the first columns were available for conditioning on September 15th. The plant was substantially complete two months later, with the first product being removed October 31, 1944.

The initial stages of the operation of the S-50 plant were far from smooth. For security reasons, Groves wanted Ferguson to operate the plant, but there was a paucity of qualified personnel in the local workforce. To train operators, the company sent four of its personnel and 10 enlisted men to Philadelphia to be trained by Phil and his group. On September 2nd, however, an explosion in the uranium fluoride transfer room wrecked a large part of the plant. In the operation of the liquid thermal diffusion plant, the UF_6 was transferred under a pressure of 1550 pounds per square inch to the diffusion columns. Because UF_6 was such a toxic substance, these high-pressure reservoirs were all located in a separate room called the transfer room. That afternoon there were three men working in the transfer room. One of them, an enlisted soldier named Arnold Kramish, survived and told the following story:

> There were three of us in the transfer room at the time—myself and two civilians, Peter N. Bragg, Jr. of Fayetteville, Arkansas and Douglas P. Meigs of Owing Mills, Maryland. We inhaled large quantities of uranium compounds and suffered whole body acid burns. Peter and Douglas, both of them civilian engineers, died soon thereafter.[17]
>
> Four other civilians and four other soldiers were injured in the blast. Abelson even took in several caustic lungfuls of the stuff but did not need hospitalization.

Phil wrote Meig's widow that his "memories of this tragic accident" were "the saddest and the bitterest that I know and will remain so the rest of my life."

---

[17]Kramish, Arnold. Hiroshima's First Victims. *Rocky Mountain News*, Aug 6, 1995, p. 93A. Also, Amato, Ivan. *Pushing the Horizon, Seventy-Five Years of High Stakes Science and Technology at the Naval Research Laboratory*; U.S. Government Printing Office: Washington, DC, 1998.

The liquid thermal diffusion plant at Oak Ridge,
Tennessee (National Archives).

Nonetheless, Phil was unwilling to disclose what his workers were doing to any of the emergency workers called to the scene. The following statement (part of an FBI clearance investigation) was reported as having been made by one of the personnel at the Philadelphia plant:

> . . . [H]e recalled Dr. Abelson as a former worker for the Naval Research Laboratory, who worked on a special project at the Naval Base during World War II. . . . Abelson kept information regarding the project so well guarded that even top Naval officials at the base were unaware of the exact nature of his project.

Another respondent "cited the episode in which there was an accident on the project in which the lives of certain workers were endangered. The workers were immediately taken to the Naval Hospital nearby, but Abelson refused to release information to the hospital officials regarding the nature of the injury. It was necessary for a doctor to be dispatched from Oak Ridge, Tennessee to the Naval Hospital to treat the workers."

Kramish reported that "for decades the families of Peter Bragg and Douglas Meigs never knew how they died." Finally in 1993, Meigs, who was a civilian Navy employee, was awarded posthumously the Meritorious Civilian Service Award.

Eventually Phil and 15 of his staff moved to Oak Ridge and they eventually helped to make the plant functional. It must have been hellish to work in this plant, though, because great quantities of high-pressure steam leaked from the column fittings in the first runs. They worked in the midst of the shrieking noise of escaping steam in a forest of 48-foot columns shrouded in hot vapor.

At the liquid thermal diffusion plants in Oak Ridge and Philadelphia, ^{235}U was enriched from 0.715% to 0.86%. This product, when fed into the electromagnetic plant, increased its production rate by about 20% and improved the purity of the product.

> In October, 1944 only 10.5 pounds of enriched uranium was produced in the S-50 plant but by November it was 172 pounds and by February, 1945 3158 pounds were produced. A high of 12,730 pounds was produced in June. This material fed the electromagnetic plant and later the gaseous diffusion plant producing sufficient material for the first uranium bomb.[18]

---

[18]Jones, Vincent C. *Manhattan: The Army and the Atomic Bomb*; Center of Military History, U.S. Government Printing Office: Washington, DC, 1985; Chapter VIII (The Liquid Thermal Diffusion Process).

By April 1945, ^{235}U from Oak Ridge and plutonium from Hanford were being produced in sufficient quantities for bombs to be assembled in Los Alamos. A plutonium bomb was successfully tested at Alamogordo, New Mexico on July 16th. The uranium bomb was dropped on Hiroshima August 6th. Unfortunately the Japanese did not surrender, so a plutonium bomb was dropped on Nagasaki three days later.[19] This ended the war. The building of the atomic bomb had been a race against time and Phil's independent decision in the dark hours of 1940 to do what he could on his own proved to be a crucial.

Ross Gunn, in testimony before the Senate Committee on Atomic Energy in 1945, said, "We were credited with shortening the war by a week or more, in spite of the delaying tactics and fumbling politics imposed on us by some members of the Manhattan project."[20]

I know that Phil was proud of that contribution, but did he, like some of the other Manhattan Project scientists, have moral qualms about his role in the construction of the atomic bomb? He didn't write about this subject and I didn't talk to him about it, but in her interview more than 50 years later Amy Crumpton did:

> Crumpton: "So, I want to ask your reactions to the events of August of 1945. After the dropping of the bomb, many scientists, many physicists in particular, had concerns about its use and the new uses of atomic energy. I was wondering if you had any thoughts you'd like to share with me on that or if you had shared any of their concerns at the time about what we were getting ourselves into with this new technology?"

> Phil: "Well, as it turned out, I knew one of the people involved in planning for the invasion of Japan. It was his feeling that there

---

[19]In Hiroshima 66,000 were killed, in Nagasaki 39,000.
[20]Testimony to the Senate Committee on Atomic Energy. See footnote 8.

would have been very massive U.S. and Japanese casualties.[21] So, from the standpoint of casualties overall, my impression was that there were less casualties as it happened than had conventional warfare gone on. There's no way that you can guarantee what is going to happen in future when a new technology is released, whether it's going to be beneficial to a lot of people or whether it's going to be harmful. History tells me that in every generation, on average there's some damn big war. My guess would be that if it hadn't been for the restraint of the Cold War we would have had another world war. For some stupid reason people are out to kill each other."

Crumpton: "In the years after the war, a number of scientists called for test bans and control of atomic energy. Were you in any way involved in those kinds of discussions or interested in what they were doing?"

Phil: "I didn't. That was for them, I was busy about something else."

---

[21] The Secretary of War's estimate was 400,000 to 800,000 U.S. fatalities and five to ten million Japanese fatalities. Frank, Richard B. *Downfall: The End of the Imperial Japanese Empire*; Random House: New York, 1999.

7

The Forgotten Father of the Atomic Submarine

After the war, Phil and Ross Gunn returned to the Navy's original goal for the atomic-energy program, the design of an atomic submarine. Gunn had proposed the concept of an atomic submarine shortly after he heard (in person) the first account of fission from Bohr and Fermi at the Georgetown meeting in 1939.

> The general engineering characteristics of a heat-producing "fission chamber," which would generate steam to operate a high-pressure steam turbine, was outlined to him. I recall telling Admiral Bowen that I never expected seriously to propose such a fantastic program to a responsible Navy representative; but here was the proposal, and we needed $1500 to explore with the help of a chemist some of the more difficult aspects connected with the problems of isotope separation on a grand scale. Because of the Admiral's foresight, we left his office with the small allotment and were actively working on the large-scale production methods for uranium hexafluoride within a week. This was the first active work within the government on the problems of nuclear power.[1]

---

[1] Gunn, Ross. *The Early History of the Atomic Powered Submarine at the U.S. Naval Research Laboratory March 1939 to March 1946;* American Institute of Physics Neils Bohr Library, College Park, MD.

By the end of the war, the isotope-separation problem had been solved; in fact, the Philadelphia plant could have supplied the Navy's initial requirement for enriched uranium.

In August of 1944, General Leslie R. Groves, who was the head of the Manhattan District, appointed a committee to make recommendations for a postwar policy on the development of atomic energy. The chairman of this committee was Dr. R. C. Tolman, vice-chairman of the National Defense Research Committee, and the military representative on the committee was Rear Admiral Earle W. Mills, assistant chief of the Bureau of Ships.

In November of 1944, the Tolman Committee visited the Naval Research Laboratory and interviewed Rear Admiral A. H. Van Keuren (then the director of the lab), Ross Gunn, and me. The three of us vigorously presented reasons as to why a nuclear-powered submarine was needed. We pointed out that a surfaced or partially submerged submarine could easily be detected with the present radars and that the need for extended submerged operation was imperative.

The Tolman Committee was impressed with these discussions and, in its final report in December of 1944, urged the government "to initiate and push, as an urgent project, research and development studies to provide power from nuclear sources for the propulsion of naval vessels."

Soon after the atomic-bomb explosions at Hiroshima and Nagasaki in August of 1945, Gunn and I were permitted to have access to information about nuclear reactors. In early September, we visited the installations at Hanford. During the autumn of 1945, I spent several months at Oak Ridge, where I participated in two chain-reaction experiments with isotopically enriched uranium. One of these was a test to determine whether highly enriched UF_6 would go critical if tanks containing it were packed closely together. The uranium was assembled cautiously with provisions to instantly stop the reactor, if necessary. When the pile was about the size of a three-foot cube, the counters began to chatter with increased frequency, indicating that the pile had gone slightly critical. Later I participated in a test of a critical assembly of enriched uranium moderated by heavy water (D_2O). The D_2O we used had cost several million dollars. Had the wrong valve been opened, those millions of dollars would have gone down the drain. The tank containing the critical assembly was about four feet in diameter and six feet high.

In the course of the experiments on critical assemblages, our attitude was carefree, even casual. We had had a discussion ahead of time about procedures, including emergency actions, but there was no tension during the assembly of the piles. No safety officer was present. We were counting on the fact that the delayed neutrons of fission would give us as much as 30 seconds to take action.

In May 1946, however, Lewis Slotin at Los Alamos was conducting a criticality experiment when a screwdriver slipped that was separating two chunks of highly enriched fissionable material.

The assemblage went highly critical and Slotin suffered a radiation exposure that led shortly to his death. That was the end of carefree critical assemblages at Oak Ridge.

I shudder to imagine the doses of radiation that Phil must have received before the full realization of the dangers of radioactivity were known. That he lived until the age of 90 attests to the robust nature of his DNA-repair systems.

During this period Phil spent quite a lot of time at Oak Ridge, but there was a shortage of housing there, so he and his associate, Chad Raseman, stayed with Harry and Ellen Weaver in their two-bedroom pre-fab house. Both of the Weavers had worked with Phil in the thermal liquid diffusion plant and remained in Oak Ridge through 1946. As a contribution to the household and their circle of friends, Phil would routinely arrive in Oak Ridge (a dry county) with two suitcases, one containing his clothes and one containing bourbon. This made him quite popular.[2] The Weavers were the only associates of Phil's during the 1930s and 40s that I was able to interview. Ellen went on to obtain a Ph.D. in genetics and did early work on Chlamodomonas genetics, whereas Harry, a physicist, was an early employee of Hewlett–Packard.

Ellen Weaver remembers:

Chad and Phil devoted themselves to the design of the submarine. Harry and I continued with our six-day-a-week jobs, I cooked, everyone helped with the housecleaning, laundry, dishes, etc. I remember Phil helping to wring out sheets in the kitchen

------

[2] In their thorough investigations of Phil, the FBI found an Oak Ridge police record that reported a warning citation for carrying liquor in a government car.

sink—no Laundromats—and hanging them outside to dry. We played pinochle when they wanted a break. The weather was cold, rainy, and there was mud everywhere, but we were cozy and comfortable in our little house. I pored over the drawings, with little comprehension of their significance.

After the Hiroshima and Nagasaki bombs that ended the war, the American public became alarmed, almost hysterical, about anything "nuclear." Indeed, a bill was introduced into the Senate by Senator May[3] which provided severe penalties for anyone who revealed what the public supposed was "the secret" of the atomic bomb. We scientists instantly became politically active (I had never paid much attention to politics), and set about trying to educate the public about nuclear energy. Since Phil was spending a fair amount of time with us, we talked about what could be done to defuse this hysteria. His great idea was that we must demonstrate that nuclear energy could be used for something other than bombs, such as a submarine.

In the interval between August 1945 and May 1946, I spent part time at the Naval Research Laboratory designing the atomic submarine. Robert Ruskin and Chad Raseman dealt with the mechanical engineering aspects. Commander Robert J. Olsen, a submariner, was attached to the laboratory during this period and he had access to blueprints of the German advanced Walter

---

[3] Ellen Weaver is referring to a bill offered by Senators May and Johnson in 1945 that proposed a peacetime Atomic Energy Commission largely controlled by the military but with some civilian participation. Many scientists opposed this bill because of the military control it envisioned and because it proposed a penalty of 10 years in prison and a $100,000 fine for security violations. Ultimately this bill was dropped and a substitute bill offered by Connecticut Senator Brien McMahon was passed in 1946 by both houses of Congress. This set up the Atomic Energy Commission, which took over control of research and development of atomic energy with substantial civilian control.

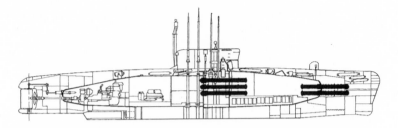

Drawing of the German Type 26 Walter submarine.

Type 26 submarine. This vessel, the most advanced submarine of the time, was capable of a submerged speed of 26–30 knots. It had diesel engines and a large tonnage of storage batteries. Although the hull design could probably have been improved to obtain higher speeds, it was decided to proceed with this hull design and to replace the diesel/storage battery power system with an atomic reactor on a weight-for-weight basis.

Thermal energy generated in the atomic pile would be transferred to liquid sodium–potasssium (KNa) alloy recirculated through the pile. This heat would drive a steam turbine. Though KNa had been previously considered as a heat exchanger, it had not been used. It had the advantageous properties, though, of a high heat capacity and a boiling temperature of 1400 °C. KNa was highly reactive with water, however, and the system had to

---

[4] KNa was later used extensively as a heat exchanger in nuclear reactors.

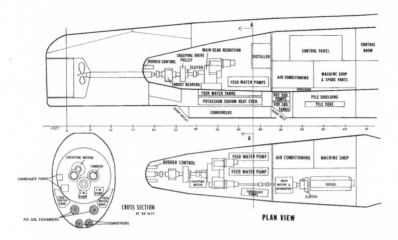

Schematic design for the power installation in the atomic submarine.

be designed to relieve the hydrogen pressure that would be generated in the event of a leak during heat exchange.[4]

The pile, together with its shielding and the KNa heat exchanger, were to be located outside the pressure hull along the keel of the submarine. It was unnecessary for the pile to be a cube and could conform to the streamline shape of the hull. This arrangement allowed for convenient maintenance and replacement in drydock. In all, about 400,000 pounds of fuel and equipment could be removed from the Walter submarine to be replaced with 270,000 pounds in the atomic submarine, including 230,000 pounds of core together with shielding. Thus, the atomic submarine could be 130,000 pounds more buoyant than the traditional diesel submarine.

The results of this study were compiled and circulated in a report entitled "Atomic Energy Submarine" by Philip Abelson, Robert Ruskin, and Chad Raseman, dated March 28, 1946.

The submarine community was then briefed on this plan. Vice-Admiral Charles Lockwood, who had commanded U.S submarines in the Pacific during World War II, recalled one of those briefings:

> If I live to be a hundred, I shall never forget that meeting on March 28, 1946. In a large Bureau of Ships conference room, its walls lined with blackboards which, in turn, were covered with diagrams, blueprints, figures and equations which Phil used to illustrate various points as he read from his document, the first ever submitted anywhere on nuclear powered subs. It sounded like something out of Jules Verne's *Twenty Thousand Leagues Under the Sea*.[5]

After submitting the submarine report, activities at the NRL that were related to isotope separation and submarine propulsion were gradually curtailed. The costly, large-scale gaseous diffusion plant at Oak Ridge became markedly successful. Activities at the Philadelphia isotope separation plant were terminated. In January 1947, the chief of Naval Operations, Fleet Admiral Chester W. Nimitz, approved a program for the design and development of nuclear power plants for submarines. In effect, this

---

[5] Polmar, Norman; Moore, K. J. *Cold War Submarines: The Design and Construction of U.S. and Soviet Submarines*; Brassey's Inc.: Washington, DC, 2004; p. 53.

was the first authoritative statement of a Navy operational requirement for nuclear propulsion in submarines.

The next key actor in the nuclear propulsion of submarines was Captain—later Vice-Admiral—Hyman Rickover. He headed a Navy team that was sent to Oak Ridge in the summer of 1946.

Rickover led a successful program aimed at developing reliable nuclear reactors. The submarine *Nautilus*, powered by one of them, was launched in late 1954. Submarines designed and built under Rickover's leadership were remarkably effective. They had an important role in safeguarding America during the Cold War.

———————————

Rickover sought and received most of the credit for developing the atomic submarine, but later Phil was called "the forgotten father of the atomic submarine."[6]

———————————

[6] In 1963, Representative Charles S. Gubser of California introduced a Congressional resolution intended to honor the "true fathers of the nuclear submarine program." The resolution expressed the thanks of the American people to Dr. Ross Gunn and Dr. Philip H. Abelson for their pioneering work on nuclear energy and nuclear propulsion while at the Naval Research Laboratory from 1939 to 1945. Baldwin, Hanson. *The New York Times*, Dec 28, 1963.

8

New Directions

While there is much more to Uncle Phil's story—he was only 33 years old at this point—there is convincing evidence that he considered his work in nuclear physics his great accomplishment. Consider the following excerpt from an interview with Amy Crumpton of the Library of Congress:

> Amy Crumpton: "We've gotten through the war years and you're at Carnegie. . . . We'll pick up when you become . . . President of Carnegie and . . . when you become Editor of *Science*. That'll probably be our most important discussion next time."

> Phil: "Well, I'll give thought as to what I should chat about . . . but it won't have the whammy of some of those earlier things."

> Crumpton: "Oh, I think there's gonna be plenty of whammy. . . . "

Phil and Ross Gunn had worked smoothly with Naval personnel during the war, but after the war, with the military services disbanding, the collegial spirit between officers and civilians disappeared, too. After their report on the atomic submarine had been submitted, both left the Navy, Phil in 1946 to return to the

Carnegie Institution of Washington and Gunn in 1947 to work at the Weather Bureau.

D uring the early months of 1946 the Navy Department was preoccupied with a coming test at Bikini Atoll in which several naval vessels were to be exposed to the explosion of an atomic bomb. I privately thought that the outcome of the project would only be a mess. I also noted that the Navy in peacetime was far different from the Navy at war. Hence, with the submission of the nuclear submarine feasibility report, I felt it was time to consider my postwar career.

I knew that nuclear physicists would be building bigger and bigger machines in their goal of attaining higher and higher energies. Ernest Lawrence had invited me to return to Berkeley, for example, but I decided that high-energy physics was not for me. Then Merle Tuve, who had been named director at the Department of Terrestrial Magnetism, invited me to meet with him. We concluded that the next great frontier would be molecular biology and that physicists could potentially have a seminal role in it. This was the kind of idea that I could get enthusiastic about, so I rejoined the staff of the DTM in September 1946 as chairman of the biophysics section.

At the Department of Terrestrial Magnetism, Phil joined a group of physicists, who like many other physicists at the time, agreed that biology was the next great problem to solve. The group at Carnegie included Richard Roberts, Phil, Ellis Bolton, Dean Cowie, and Roy Britten. This group took an early and very original approach to the problem of biosynthesis in *Escherichia coli*, which only in this period was being accepted as the model system for working out the problems of biochemistry and genetics at a fundamental level. Applying some of the first uses of isotopic tracers and paper chromatographic separation of small molecules, they worked out many of the biosynthetic pathways (e.g., those of amino acids) in *E. coli*. This work was compiled in a book published by the Carnegie Institution entitled *Biosynthesis in Escherichia coli* which became the bible for microbiologists and biochemists of that period and for some time after.

In 1953 the Carnegie Institution appointed Phil director of the Geophysical Laboratory and his intellectual interests took a new direction.[1] He initiated his own research program at the Geophysical Laboratory, a geochemical study of biological molecules in fossils, which is still a hot area of research some 50 years later.

From 1962 to 1984 Phil was editor of *Science* and in that capacity wrote more than 600 editorials on subjects as diverse as the space program, energy policy, biotechnology, and the funding of science. These editorials were well researched, often the result of wide consultation on the telephone, and were first written long hand at the kitchen table and then typed. They were concise and clear in no small part because Neva was the typist and final editor.

---

[1] This switch to geology represents the most convincing evidence of Uncle Phil's breadth as a scientist. He never had a course in geology and yet on arriving at the Geophysical Laboratory he began original work in geology and became the editor of the *Journal of Geophysical Research*. He also hired a number of great geologists.

At the Geophysical Laboratory Phil prepares a sample for the analysis of fossil biomolecules.

Phil continued his association with *Science* until a few months before his death in 2004 at age 91 and was at his office daily keeping up with new developments and writing editorials.

From 1971 to 1978 he was president of the Carnegie Institution of Washington and served on its board until his death in 2004. Thus, Phil was associated with the Carnegie Institution for 65 years.

Epilogue

Well, that brings us to the end of the story I wanted to tell, but there is a little more to say. Uncle Phil wrote his story, but he was characteristically taciturn and much was left unspoken. I have attempted to fill in the blanks. I was his nephew, though, and not a dispassionate historian. How did I experience Uncle Phil?

I didn't know Uncle Phil well as a child. I had perhaps met him only a few times before I was 21. One of those times was presumably at the double funeral in 1955 of my father and my grandmother, but those memories are clouded and I can't remember. The testiness of my interjection when he describes himself as the favored son ("I was the fair-haired boy and he [my father] was often in bad odor") must have come through. But even if I didn't know him, I knew what he had done. I could look it up in the *Encyclopedia Britannica*. He was certainly a role model for me.

Like my grandfather, my father, and Uncle Phil before me, I went to Washington State College. I didn't even apply anywhere else. And like them all, I started out in engineering, but unlike my father and my grandfather, I quickly realized that engineering was not for me. For one thing, I got a "D" in mechanical drawing, because unlike all the other students in the course, my drawings were smudged and ugly, whereas theirs were crisp and beautiful. Instead, like Phil, I decided to major in physics, though perhaps it was only to prove myself to Phil that I chose physics over English.

Another reason I chose physics was that I loved the sophomore physics course taught by Paul Anderson. Anderson, who as a young man had been Phil's professor, was now much older, but

131

Harold (left) and Phil, 1953, behind the family home
in Tacoma.

he was still making the same insightful hunches about where science was going that he had done during Phil's time. I first heard
about the double-helical structure of DNA in a thermodynamics
course that Anderson gave, in which he discussed neg-entropy
and the information in DNA sequences. And, like all of the other
physicists of the day, I was led to read Erwin Schrödinger's *What
is Life?*. This was just five years after the Watson–Crick structure
and long before any biologist at Washington State knew what

was happening. Furthermore, Anderson, a solid-state physicist, had by this time begun doing molecular biology in his lab in the basement of the physics building. After my senior year, I spent the summer in his lab trying to synchronize cultures of *E. coli* harboring the bacteriophage lambda prophage and to measure induction as a function of time during the division cycle.

I had applied to biophysics programs for graduate school and had decided to go to the Department of Biophysics at Johns Hopkins. I arrived there in the fall of 1960 (my first trip to the east coast) and my first interaction there with Uncle Phil was to give an impromptu seminar to the biophysics group that he led at the Department of Terrestrial Magnetism of the Carnegie Institution of Washington. This was a wonderful group of scientists who all worked in the lab and had lunch together. The group included Richard Roberts, who had done one of the first experiments to confirm nuclear fission (Chapter 4), and a number of other physicists who, because of the contributions they made during that exciting postwar period in biology, will be familiar names to most biologists of my generation. As I remember that afternoon, there were only the five of them there at that time. In addition to Phil and Roberts, they were Dean Cowie, Ellis Bolton, and Roy Britten. I was intimidated by the barrage of questions that I got, but excited to be participating (for the first time) in the real world of science. Phil had ushered me into that world.

It was really during that five years at Johns Hopkins (1960–1965) that I got to know Uncle Phil. Especially during the first years, before my marriage, I would often join Phil on the Metroliner in Baltimore on Friday afternoons as he traveled home from Washington to Philadelphia for the weekend. On the train we would talk about science, and in Philadelphia we would play bridge nonstop with my Aunt Neva and my very bright cousin Ellen. Then Phil and I would return on Monday morning.

Sometimes in the summer we would pack a lunch and go to Atlantic City for the horse races. Both Neva and Phil loved to go to the track, but they had completely different betting styles. Neva, who had grown up in the country (in Colfax near Washington State), and was a physician, could tell what a horse could do by things as subtle as its sweat patterns after the warm-up. Phil, on the other hand, would bet the smart money. This meant watching the pari-mutuel board and calculating the odds himself during the pre-race period. He was looking for a step-discontinuity in the odds indicating that someone had bet a lot of money on a horse. This often happened at the last moment, so Phil would wait until then and race down to the betting window to place his bet. Both methods worked at times.

In this period we formed a lasting bond. After graduate school, I spent three years at the MRC Laboratory of Molecular Biology in Cambridge, England. At the time, this was the center of things in molecular biology, just as Lawrence's lab had been, in Phil's time, the center of experimental nuclear physics. After Cambridge, I got my first job in the Department of Chemistry at the University of California, San Diego. Again, the connections with Phil's career continued. My space in Bonner Hall was carved out of Martin Kamen's lab and Martin became a mentor to me. Kamen had been a post-doctoral fellow with Phil in Lawrence's lab and they had spent many nights together running the cyclotron. Also in our department at that time was Harold Urey, who had reviewed the NRL program in 1943. Urey, then in his 80s, was still very sharp.

In 1988 my brother Roy and I bought a cabin on Priest Lake in northern Idaho and Phil chipped in to help us buy it. Every year, until just before his death, he would come out in the summer for one or two weeks. He loved being at Priest Lake.

Uncle Phil at Upper Priest Lake, 2001.

We fished together, picked huckleberries, and canoed. Every morning he went on a five-mile run, which may help to explain why he lived so long. When there was a free moment we would play cribbage, unless four could be found for bridge, and when together, as in the long periods in the boat with no bites, we constantly talked about science. But it was always about current or future science (during much of this period Phil was editor of *Science*) and never about those epochal days of the 1930s and 40s. How I wish now that I had started this project 20 years ago when I could have questioned not only Uncle Phil but also his colleagues. At the time I was too busy, though, and besides, Phil didn't really want to talk about the past, especially not about what had been a secret.

Today, with this project now as complete as I can make it, I think I know more about what he accomplished than he ever would have told me. Unfortunately, though, I still have only the faintest glimmer of what his life was really like as day after day, with the threat of what Germany could possibly do hanging over their heads, he and his small group of colleagues made liquid thermal diffusion work.

I am sitting on the bench in our garden near the tea house on a warm May afternoon looking out across San Francisco Bay to Berkeley and I wish that Uncle Phil were sitting beside me. He would be able to fairly closely spot where the physics lab was, where he lived with Neva, how the ferry would have run to San Francisco (there was no bridge then), and where in the city he and Neva had run into the Braun-Knecht and Heimann scientific supply store on that fateful day when he spent his suit money on uranium. Perhaps he wouldn't have dwelled on any of those things. But I do know that he would have been enthusiastic about a suggestion to go down to the kitchen to play some cribbage.

John Abelson, San Francisco
May 14, 2006

Bibliography

Amato, Ivan. Pushing the Horizon: *Seventy-five Years of High Stakes Science and Technology at the Naval Research Laboratory*; U.S. Government Printing Office: Washington, DC, 1996.

Bird, Kai; Sherwin, Martin J. American Prometheus: *The Triumph and Tragedy of J. Robert Oppenheimer*; Alfred A. Knopf: New York, 2005.

Bowen, Harold G. Ships Machinery and Mossbacks: *The Autobiography of a Naval Engineer*; Princeton University Press: Princeton, NJ, 1954.

Childs, Herbert. *An American Genius: The Life of Ernest Orlando Lawrence, Father of the Cyclotron*; E. P. Dutton & Co.: New York, 1968.

Christman, Al. *Target Hiroshima: Deak Parsons and the Creation of the Atomic Bomb*; Naval Institute Press: Annapolis, MD, 1998.

Groves, Leslie M. *Now It Can Be Told: The Story of the Manhattan Project*; Harper & Brothers Publishers: New York, 1962.

Bernstein, Jeremy. Oppenheimer: *Portrait of an Enigma*; Ivan R. Dee: Chicago, IL, 2004.

Howes, Ruth H.; Herzenberg, Caroline L. *Their Day in the Sun: Women of the Manhattan Project*; Temple University Press: Philadelphia, PA, 1999.

Kamen, Martin. *Radiant Science, Dark Politics: A Memoir of the Nuclear Age*; University of California Press: Berkeley, CA, 1985.

Rhodes, Richard. *The Making of the Atomic Bomb*; Simon & Schuster: New York, 1986.

Smyth, Henry DeWolf. *Atomic Energy for Military Purposes: The Official Report on the Development of the Atomic Bomb Under the Auspices of the United States Government, 1940–1945*; Princeton University Press: Princeton, NJ, 1945.

Uys, Errol Lincoln. *Riding the Rails: Teenagers on the Move During the Great Depression*; Routledge: New York, 2003.

Wilson, Jane, Ed. *All In Our Time: The Reminiscences of Twelve Nuclear Pioneers*; The Bulletin of the Atomic Scientists: Chicago, IL, 1975.